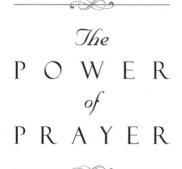

The
POWER
of
PRAYER

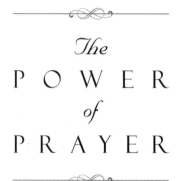

The

POWER

of

PRAYER

EDITED BY DALE SALWAK

INTRODUCTION BY NEALE DONALD WALSCH

NEW WORLD LIBRARY
NOVATO, CALIFORNIA

New World Library
14 Pamaron Way
Novato, CA 94949

Cover design: Mary Ann Casler
Text design: Mary Ann Casler and Aaron Kenedi
Editorial: Becky Benenate

Library of Congress Cataloging-in-Publication Data

The power of prayer / edited by Dale Salwak.
p.   cm.
ISBN 1-57731-123-X (alk. paper)
1. Prayer. I. Salwak, Dale.

BL560.P66   1998   98-24991
291.4'3 — dc21   CIP

First Paperback Printing, November 1999
Printed in Canada on acid-free paper
ISBN 1-57731-123-X
Disributed by Publishers Group West
10 9 8 7 6 5 4 3 2 1

To our families and friends

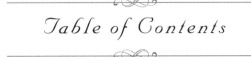

Table of Contents

Acknowledgments

*Q*uite obviously this book is a joint endeavor. I am enormously indebted to the contributors, many of whom took valuable time away from their own work and busy lives to participate; and to Becky Benenate, editorial director at New World Library, whose wise counsel has been a valued gift. Without her enthusiasm and dedication every step of the way, there would be no book.

Preface

DALE SALWAK

God does nothing but by prayer,
and everything with it.
— JOHN WESLEY

These words, written more than 250 years ago by the founder of the Methodist Church, bear witness to the central conviction of this book: There is extraordinary power in prayer.

Testimony to this simple truth comes from every era, every belief system, and every varied niche of the human experience. Consider, for example, the evangelist D. L. Moody, who wrote, "Every great moment of history can be traced to a kneeling figure." Or Ole Hallesby, who called prayer "the conduit through which power from heaven is brought to earth." Indeed, prayer is a mighty instrument, affirms William Law, "not for getting man's will done in heaven," but "for getting God's will done on earth."

The apostle James assures us, "The earnest prayers of a righteous person have great power and wonderful results."

Tragically, however, too few people have ever learned how to put prayer to work for them. "We have no sense of coming earnestly and expectantly to God," says Billy Graham; "we simply use prayer as a formality."

But as this book makes abundantly clear, genuine prayer is not a formality, nor is it a dreary obligation, a psychological trick, superfluous introspection, or merely wishful thinking. Above all, prayer is not just a vague spiritual pantomime, an unthinking rote exercise of mindless grumbling, vain repetition, or even magical incantation.

What, then, is prayer? It is a way to make contact with God, to feel His presence even more surely. "I can take my telescope and look millions and millions of miles into space," said Sir Isaac Newton, "but I can lay it aside and go into my room, shut the door, get down on my knees in earnest prayer, and see more of heaven and get closer to God than I can assisted by all the telescopes and material agencies on earth."

The rabbis called prayer "the service of the heart." It has also been variously defined as the interior life; a way of loving others; an intimate, ongoing interaction with God; a request; or a petition. Augustine defined prayer as a turning of the mind and heart to God: "True, whole prayer," he wrote, "is nothing but love." Prayer, said John Vianney, "is the inner bath of love into which the soul plunges itself."

For our purposes, perhaps the most apt description is that which a child might use: the soul talking with God. If we want to have intimate fellowship with God, and if we want to know the whole will of God and to experience fully the transforming power of His presence in our lives — then we must talk to Him and we must listen. We must reveal ourselves and our doubts and fears, we must ask our questions, and affirm our faith. We must pray to explore our own souls and to realize the wonder of His love.

And what a privilege it is to enter into the very presence of that love! We do so, says A. W. Tozer, "because, and only because, He has first put an urge within us that spurs us to the pursuit." If that is accurate, and I believe it is, then it was His "still, small voice," blended with my mother's, that urged me forward as a child in my own prayerful life.

I began by learning the Lord's Prayer, which I recited every night with my mother after I was tucked safely into bed with the lights off. In the dark I couldn't see her, but I could feel her reassuring presence and hear her soft, loving, confident tones as she began, "Our Father, which art in Heaven. . . . "

In time, I was able to commit the words to memory, and soon they became my constant companion in every conceivable setting. Later, she encouraged me to memorize some of the Psalms, starting with the Twenty-third: "The Lord is my shepherd, I shall not want, . . ." Those words, too, went deep into my mind and heart to become my own, informing and shaping my spontaneous expressions of prayer as I learned to voice my innermost concerns and desires with confidence and submission. "No matter what you're doing," my mother would say, "you can pray — anywhere, at anytime."

How often since then have I realized the truth of her confidence! No matter is too small or too great to be of concern to God, but first we must bring it before His throne of grace. God intervenes in all areas of life. Even in activity, when we are grounded in prayer, we become more efficient, more creative, and more energized. "Every one of us needs half an hour of prayer each day," wrote Francis de Sales, "except when we are busy — then we need an hour."

Although seen from a variety of traditions and perspectives, this same confidence and trust resonates through the essays that follow. The purpose of these writers and their shared thoughts is not necessarily to prescribe, but to encourage, console, and even inspire. As they make clear, the power of prayer is based on a very specific conception of God as one who loves us unconditionally. "O love that will not let me go," wrote hymn lyricist George Matheson. The desire to experience God, to get beyond merely knowing about Him to truly loving Him, is the very essence of genuine prayer.

But I am sure the contributors will agree when I say that there is a huge difference between *knowing about* prayer and actually *knowing* prayer. On this the Rule of Benedict is clear: "If a man wants to pray, let him go and pray." Prayer should be our first resource, someone once said, not our last resort. And as Frank Biano writes, "It's a powerful force, prayer is. God help anyone, or anything, that tries to stand in its way."

Introduction

NEALE DONALD WALSCH

Your Life Is Your Prayer

*P*rayer is the most important part of the human experience. It is the most important part of our daily activities. The *reason* it is the most important part of our experience and our activities is because it is the process by which we create our lives. It should be understood by anyone examining the subject of prayer that everything we think, see, and do is a prayer. Life is a prayer in the sense that it is a continuous request to the universe and its God to present us with what we choose and desire.

God understands our desires not just through the occasional utterances that we call "prayers" in the traditional sense, but through every thought we think, every word we speak, and everything we do. Our thoughts, our words, and our actions are our prayers. Most people do not think of life as a constant prayer; most people believe they are praying only when involved in that deliberate, peculiar activity we know as prayer. Thus, many people feel that their prayers either go unanswered or are answered sporadically and only in the affirmative. But the truth is, prayer does not begin with kneeling down, or lighting a votive candle, or sitting in meditation, or picking up our prayer beads, or performing some outward or inner ritual.

Prayer begins at the moment of our birth and ends with our death, if we speak in the classic terms of most human understanding. Of course, if we move beyond the notions of birth and death to reach higher understandings, we learn that birth and death are merely the beginning and the end of an ongoing, cyclical experience through which we move throughout the ages and for all time.

But in normal human terms, in our relative world, I would use the word "prayer" to create a greater understanding among a larger number of people. Our prayer begins within the moment of our birth in this particular lifetime. And at our death this particular version of our prayer ends. But at no time between our birth and our death do we cease our prayer.

If we understood that every word, thought, and action was a prayer sent right to God, a request sent right to the Heavens, I believe we would change much of what we think, say, and do. Further, I believe we would better understand why our more formalized prayers seem to be answered only sporadically, if at all. For here is what really happens: In our formalized prayers we seek God's intercession or intervention in our affairs, hoping that God will somehow alter or create something for us. Yet these *formal* prayers only take a moment or two each day, or for some, each week. The rest of our time — probably 95 to 99 percent — is spent sending, oftentimes unwittingly, prayers to God that work exactly in the opposite direction of our formal prayers.

So we pray for one thing and we go out and do another. Or we pray for one thing and we go out and think another. Let me give you a typical example. We may pray for greater abundance in our life, or for help with a financial problem. Those prayers are earnestly offered, earnestly said, and earnestly sent to God during our formal, ritualized time for prayer. Then for the rest of the week we go around harboring thoughts of insufficiency, saying words of insufficiency, and demonstrating insufficiency in the everyday actions of our lives. So 95 percent of the time we send prayers that affirm we don't have enough and 5 percent of the time we ask God to bring us enough. It is very difficult for the universe to grant us our wishes when 95 percent of the time we are, in fact, asking for something else.

This is the single most misunderstood aspect of prayer in our human experience. This truth is that the universe is a giant xerox, sending us, all the time, the answer to our prayers. And we are, in fact, sending prayers to the universe all the time, from morning till night, from birth till death. This is at once both empowering and, for people who are unwilling to take the responsibility it inherently creates, frightening. Only for those who understand the great gift that God has given us — the gift of our ability to create what we want — does this form of prayer seem inviting. For those unable to accept this level of responsibility for their actions, this form of prayer — morning to night, birth to death, in the shape of our words, thoughts, and actions — seems intimidating at best and unacceptable at worst.

Only when we are willing to accept that our words are creative, our thoughts are creative, and our actions are creative, could this be attractive. Many are unwilling to accept this as truth because they are not very proud of the majority of their thoughts, words, and actions and certainly don't want them to be considered as actual requests to God. And yet they are.

The injunction then is to speak, think, and act in a way of which we can be proud — in a way that sends to God our grandest thoughts and produces our highest visions and thus creates Heaven on Earth for all of us.

The thoughts expressed here are not new nor are they what one would usually think of as "new age." As a matter of fact, a wonderful minister at the Marble Cathedral in New York City named Dr. Norman Vincent Peale spoke many of these same words when he authored what is arguably one of the world's ten most famous books, *The Power of Positive Thinking*. What Dr. Peale said is what I am saying here: Your entire life is your prayer.

When we become consciously aware of this, and when we accept this truth with joy, our entire lives change — sometimes virtually overnight and other times more slowly and subtly. When we accept this truth, we suddenly understand that God is our best friend and has given us tools of unlimited power to create the reality we seek to experience.

I have had the beautiful gift of experiencing my own conversation with God, and the most urgent prayer of my life has been answered through that conversation. Every question I ever had in my life was answered in that conversation, including how best to pray. Two important points about prayer were made in that conversation. The first point is that the most powerful prayer is the prayer of gratitude. When we thank God in advance for what we wish to use and experience in our lives, we affirm that we have already received it and all that is awaiting is our *perception* of receiving it. Therefore, the power of a prayer exists in direct proportion to the degree of gratitude contained within the prayer.

The most extraordinary prayer I have ever heard is one sentence I find myself saying continually throughout my life: "Thank you God for helping me to understand that this problem has already been solved for me." This prayer has moved me through the most difficult moments in my life into peace and equanimity and even serenity.

My second major point about prayer is that *everyone* may have a conversation with God. The process by which we communicate with God and by which God communicates with us is open to all of us, not just to a select few — not to the prophets, the sages, and the wisdom bringers of all time, but to the butchers, the bakers, and the candlestick makers, and the barbers, lawyers, homemakers, politicians, teachers, and airline pilots — all of us.

God's communication with us is two-way, not one-way. God says to us that it is not necessary to pray a prayer of supplication. A prayer of supplication is a statement that we do not now have something, or we would not be asking for it. Therefore, asking for something literally pushes it away, for one does not ask for something one already has. In the request, then, is hidden our scarcity. That statement produces the result of *not having*. That is why all the great sages and all the great teachers of all the world's mystical and religious traditions, bar none, have said to pray a prayer of gratitude. Thank you, God, for allowing me to know that this problem has already been solved for me.

Then go on with your day and notice the miracle.

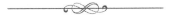

CHAPTER ONE

The Essence of Prayer

We need not perplex ourselves as to the precise mode in which prayer is answered. It is enough for us to know and feel that it is the most natural, the most powerful, and the most elevated expression of our thoughts and wishes in all great emergencies.

— A. P. STANLEY

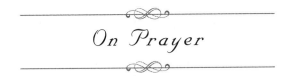

On Prayer

MOTHER TERESA

I don't think there is anyone who needs God's help and grace as much as I do. Sometimes I feel so helpless and weak. I think this is why God uses me. Because I cannot depend on my own strength, I rely on Him twenty-four hours a day. If the day had even more hours, then I would need His help and grace during those hours as well. All of us must cling to God through prayer.

My secret is very simple: I pray. Through prayer I become one in love with Christ. I realize that praying to Him is loving Him.

In reality, there is only one true prayer, only one substantial prayer: Christ Himself. There is only one voice that rises above the face of the earth: the voice of Christ. Perfect prayer does not consist in many words, but in the fervor of the desire that raises the heart to Jesus.

Love to pray. Feel the need to pray often during the day. Prayer enlarges the heart until it is capable of containing God's gift of Himself. Ask and seek and your heart will grow big enough to receive Him and keep Him as your own.

We want so much to pray properly and then we fail. We get discouraged and give up. If you want to pray better, you must pray more. God allows the failure but He does not want the discouragement. He wants us to be more childlike, more humble, more grateful in prayer, to remember we all belong to the mystical body of Christ, which is praying always.

We need to help each other in our prayers. Let us free our minds. Let's not pray long, drawn-out prayers, but let's pray short ones full of love. Let us pray on behalf of those who do not pray. Let us remember, if we want to be able to love, we must be able to pray!

Prayer that comes from the mind and heart is called mental prayer. We must never forget that we are bound toward perfection and should aim ceaselessly at it. The practice of daily mental prayer is necessary to reach that goal. Because it is the breath of life to our soul, holiness is impossible without it.

It is only by mental prayer and spiritual reading that we can cultivate the gift of prayer. Mental prayer is greatly fostered by simplicity — that is, forgetfulness of self by transcendence of the body and of our senses, and by frequent aspirations that feel our prayer. "In mental prayer," says Saint John Vianney, "shut your eyes, shut your mouth, and open your heart." In vocal prayer we speak to God; in mental prayer He speaks to us. It is then that God pours Himself into us.

Our prayers should be burning words coming forth from the furnace of hearts filled with love. In your prayers, speak to God with great reverence and confidence. Do not drag behind or run ahead; do not shout or keep silent, but devoutly, with great sweetness, with natural simplicity, without any affectation, offer your praise to God with the whole of your heart and soul.

Just once, let the love of God take entire and absolute possession of your heart; let it become to your heart like a second nature; let your heart suffer nothing contrary to enter; let it apply itself continually to increase this love of God by seeking to please Him in all things and refusing Him nothing; let it accept as from His hand everything that happens to it; let it have a firm determination never to commit any fault deliberately and knowingly or, if it should fail, to be humbled and to rise up again at once — and such a heart will pray continually.

People are hungry for the Word of God that will give peace, that will give unity, that will give joy. But you cannot give what you don't have. That's why it is necessary to deepen your life of prayer.

Be sincere in your prayers. Sincerity is humility, and you acquire humility only by accepting humiliations. All that has been said about humility is not enough to teach you humility. All that you have read about humility is not enough to teach you humility. You learn humility only by accepting humiliations. And you will meet humiliation all through your life. The greatest humiliation is to know that you are nothing. This you come to know when you face God in prayer.

Often a deep and fervent look at Christ is the best prayer: I look at Him and He looks at me. When you come face to face with God, you cannot but know that you are nothing, that you have nothing.

It is difficult to pray if you don't know how to pray, but we must help ourselves to pray. The first means to use is silence. We cannot put ourselves directly in the presence of God if we do not practice internal and external silence.

The interior silence is very difficult, but we must make the effort. In silence we will find new energy and true unity. The energy of God will be ours to do all things well, and so will the unity of our thoughts with His thoughts, the unity of our prayers with His prayers, the unity of our actions with His actions, of our life with His life. Unity is the fruit of prayer, of humility, of love.

In the silence of the heart God speaks. If you face God in prayer and silence, God will speak to you. Then you will know that you are nothing. It is only when you realize your nothingness, your emptiness, that God can fill you with Himself. Souls of prayer are souls of great silence.

Silence gives us a new outlook on everything. We need silence to be able to touch souls. The essential thing is not what we say but what God says to us and through us. In that silence, He will listen to us; there He will speak to our soul, and there we will hear His voice.

Listen in silence, because if your heart is full of other things you cannot hear the voice of God. But when you have listened to the voice of God in the stillness of your heart, then your heart is filled with God. This will need much sacrifice, but if we really mean to pray and want to pray we must be ready to do it now. These are only the first steps toward prayer but if we never make the first step with a determination, we will not reach the last one: the presence of God.

This is what we have to learn right from the beginning: to listen to the voice of God in our heart, and then in the silence of the heart God speaks. Then from the fullness of our hearts, our mouth will have to speak. That is the connection. In the silence of the heart, God speaks and you have to listen. Then in the fullness of your heart, because it is full of God, full of love, full of compassion, full of faith, your mouth will speak.

Remember, before you speak, it is necessary to listen, and only then, from the fullness of your heart you speak and God listens.

The contemplatives and ascetics of all ages and religions have sought God in the silence and solitude of the desert, forest, and mountain. Jesus Himself spent forty days in the desert and the mountains, communing for long hours with the Father in the silence of the night.

We too are called to withdraw at certain intervals into deeper silence and aloneness with God, together as a community as well as personally. To be alone with Him, not with our books, thoughts, and memories but completely stripped of everything, to dwell lovingly in His presence — silent, empty, expectant, and motionless.

We cannot find God in noise or agitation. Nature: trees, flowers, and grass grow in silence. The stars, the moon, and the sun move in silence. What is essential is not what we say but what God tells us and what He tells others through us. In silence He listens to us; in silence He speaks to our souls. In silence we are granted the privilege of listening to His voice.

Silence of our eyes.
Silence of our ears.
Silence of our mouths.
Silence of our minds.
. . . in the silence of the heart
    God will speak.

Silence of the heart is necessary so you can hear God everywhere — in the closing of the door, in the person who needs you, in the birds that sing, in the flowers, in the animals.

If we are careful of silence it will be easy to pray. There is so much talk, so much repetition, so much carrying on of tales in words and in writing. Our prayer life suffers so much because our hearts are not silent.

I shall keep the silence of my heart with greater care, so that in the silence of my heart I hear His words of comfort and from the fullness of my heart I comfort Jesus in the distressing disguise of the poor.

Real prayer is union with God, a union as vital as that of the vine to the branch, which is the illustration Jesus gives us in the Gospel of John. We need prayer. We need that union to produce good fruit. The fruit is what we produce with our hands, whether it be food, clothing, money, or something else. All of this is the fruit of our oneness with God. We need a life of prayer, of poverty, and of sacrifice to do it with love.

Sacrifice and prayer complement each other. There is no prayer without sacrifice, and there is no sacrifice without prayer. Jesus' life was spent in intimate union with His Father as He passed through the world. We need to do the same. Let's walk by His side. We need to give Christ a chance to make use of us, to be His word and His work, to share His food and His clothing in the world today.

If we do not radiate the light of Christ around us, the sense of the darkness that prevails in the world will increase.

We are called to love the world. And God loved the world so much that He gave Jesus. Today He loves the world so much that He gives you and me to be His love, His compassion, and His presence, through a life of prayer, of sacrifice, of surrender to God. The response that God asks of you is to be a contemplative.

If we take Jesus at His word, all of us are contemplatives in the heart of the world, for if we have faith, we are continually in His presence. By contemplation the soul draws directly from the heart of God the graces, which the active life must distribute. Our lives must be connected with the living Christ in us. If we do not live in the presence of God we cannot go on.

What is contemplation? To live the life of Jesus. This is what I understand. To love Jesus, to live His life in us, to live our life in His life. That's contemplation. We must have a clean heart to be able to see — no jealousy, anger, contention, and especially no uncharitableness. To me, contemplation is not to be locked in a dark place, but to allow Jesus to live His passion, His love, His humility in us, praying with us, being with us, and sanctifying through us.

Our contemplation is our life. It is not a matter of doing but being. It is the possession of our spirit by the Holy Spirit breathing into us the plenitude of God and sending us forth to the whole creation as His personal message of love.

We shall not waste our time in looking for extraordinary experiences in our life of contemplation but live by pure faith, ever watching and ready for His coming by doing our day-to-day duties with extraordinary love and devotion.

Our life of contemplation simply put is to realize God's constant presence and His tender love for us in the least little things of life. To be constantly available to Him, loving Him with our whole heart, whole mind, whole soul, and whole strength, no matter in what form He may come to us. Does your mind and your heart go to Jesus as soon as you get up in the morning? This is prayer, that you turn your mind and heart to God.

Prayer is the very life of oneness, of being one with Christ. Therefore, prayer is as necessary as the air, as the blood in our body, as anything, to keep us alive to the grace of God. To pray generously is not enough, we must pray devoutly, with fervor and piety. We must pray perseveringly and with great love. If we don't pray, our presence will have no power, our words will have no power.

We need prayers in order to better carry out the work of God, and so that in every moment we may know how to be completely available to Him.

We should make every effort to walk in the presence of God, to see God in all the persons we meet, to live our prayer throughout the day.

Knowledge of the self puts us on our knees, and it is very necessary for love. For knowledge of God produces love, and knowledge of the self produces humility. Knowledge of the self is a very important thing in our lives. As Saint Augustine says, "Fill yourselves first, and then only will you be able to give to others."

Knowledge of the self is also a safeguard against pride, especially when you are tempted in life. The greatest mistake is to think you are too strong to fall into temptation. Put your finger in the fire and it will burn. So we have to go through the fire. The temptations are allowed by God. The only thing we have to do is to refuse to give in.

Prayer, to be fruitful, must come from the heart and must be able to touch the heart of God. See how Jesus taught His disciples to pray. I believe each time we say "Our Father," God looks at His hands, where He has carved us. ("I have carved you on the palm of my hand." See Isaiah 49:16.) He looks at His hands, and He sees us there. How wonderful the tenderness and love of God!

If we pray the "Our Father," and live it, we will be holy. Everything is there: God, myself, my neighbor. If I forgive, then I can be holy and can pray. All this comes from a humble heart, and if we have this we will know how to love God, to love self, and to love our neighbor. This is not complicated, and yet we complicate our lives so much, by so many additions. Just one thing counts — to be humble, to pray. The more you pray, the better you will pray.

A child has no difficulty expressing his little mind in simple words that say so much. Jesus said to Nicodemus: "Become as a little child." If we pray the gospel, we will allow Christ to grow in us. So pray lovingly like children, with an earnest desire to love much and to make loved the one that is not loved.

All our words will be useless unless they come from within. Words that do not give the light of Christ increase the darkness. Today, more than ever, we need to pray for the light to know the will of God, for the love to accept the will of God, for the way to do the will of God.

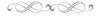

Is Anyone Listening?

ALAN C. MERMANN, M.D., M.DIV.

*P*rayer is one of the pillars that support my life. I depend upon prayer to help orient myself in this world of love and work, of anxiety and friendship, of truth known in paradox, and of death in the presence of life. Prayer is a power that cleanses as it reveals, hints at hope in despair, offers courage to confront fear, and confirms the existence of a spirit that informs as it corrects. To understand the essence of prayer we must ask a few questions: What is prayer? To what do I pray? What do I expect of prayer? What experiences have I had that confirm that there is power in prayer? Is anyone listening?

WHAT IS PRAYER?

The *Oxford English Dictionary* defines prayer as "a solemn and humble request to God, or to an object of worship; a supplication, petition, or thanksgiving, usually expressed in words." I would add the adjective, "personal," to this description of the request. So much prayer in church (that is, pastoral prayer) is a bulletin board of catastrophes, worldwide and individual, that need to be addressed by a God who is apparently unaware of events: poverty and hunger, war and politics, and diseases and accidents. God is asked to be with the sick and the suffering, bring an end to war, stop ethnic quarrels, feed the hungry, and house the homeless. I find this type of prayer to be nonsense, even sacrilege. The assumption is that God does not know or does not care; that we must remind God of problems that have been ignored or are not seen.

Prayer is, for me, exquisitely personal. It gives me a way to reflect on a study of myself in this world of grace and suffering, of unbounded gifts and overwhelming needs, of persisting love and horrifying loneliness, and of overwhelming power and weakness that can conquer.

To Which God Do I Pray?

There are a number of options available to us in choosing the image of God to whom we address prayer. As we study and learn about this amazing physical world, we are astounded by its wonder and beauty. There is a microscopic universe in which all matter is composed of energy: everything is made out of subatomic particles invisible to us. What we see is not what is really there! There is an astrophysical universe of a magnitude beyond our most fantastic imaginings in which the creation of supernovas and stars is occurring every moment. We are somewhere between the unknowable and the unbelievable. Where, in all this wonder and actual reality, is my God? Is He an attractive, although slightly frowning, elderly man with a beard who sits at a table with Jesus and the disciples while He keeps careful and accurate count of not only our acts, but our very thoughts? Is God a person in the ways I know a person to be?

Or is God an impossible composite of the biblical record? Is He the God who stopped the motion of the sun for Joshua so that the Israelites could complete the slaughter of the Amorites; the God who hardened the heart of Pharaoh so that the first-born Egyptians and their animals would die; the God who abandoned Jesus on the cross; the God who raised Jesus from the dead; the God whom we testify as being all-knowing, all-powerful, and all-present who watched the fate of the Chosen at Auschwitz; or the God who dwells within us as Spirit, the very center of life?

Or is "God" a word that encompasses, vaguely, a spirit that pervades all reality, a soul-concept that adds philosophical meaning to what we see and know, but which is not really knowable in this vast and unknowable world? Is "God" so vague a concept as to be, finally, a word *without* meaning? In my shallowness and chauvinism, I know almost nothing of the Gods that millions of other faithful people worship and declare to be central to their lives. Because of the way I was raised my ignorance of the defining and basic faiths of other religious groups is profound. Considering all the possibilities, to which God do I pray?

HELP MY UNBELIEF!

The father of the epileptic boy in the gospel of Mark is a constant companion of mine. Jesus assures the father that, for those who believe, who have faith, healing is possible. The father says, as I would, "I believe!" But then he adds, as I would, "Help my unbelief" (Mark 9:24). Many of us live in a deadlock between belief and unbelief. Underlying an ardent prayer can be the question, "Is anyone listening?" The experiences of our century with its massive blind destruction, suffering, and carnage cast doubt on the concept of a God involved in the welfare of the created universe. And yet, so many of those who died in the Holocaust of

World War II died with prayers on their lips and confidence in their hearts and minds. Who was listening to them?

HOW DO I PRAY?

Prayer can be a most difficult and trying task. To whom, or to what, do I address my prayer? What do I seek in my prayers? Am I informing my God of my needs, hoping that they will be satisfied? Am I asking for "peace on earth, good will toward men"? Do I get on my knees and close my eyes, hold beads, chant a mantra, or recite a list of miseries that need relief? Is there a formula that guarantees being heard? How often do I, should I, pray? These questions speak to our common confusions about praying, and the very nature of prayer.

The most sincere preparations for prayer are easily thwarted. John Donne, a seventeenth-century metaphysical poet, deeply religious thinker, and dean of St. Paul's Cathedral, London, speaks to the problem in a 1626 sermon he gave at the funeral of a friend:

> I throw myself down in my chamber, and I call in, and invite God, and his angels thither, and when they are there, I neglect God and his angels, for the noise of a fly, for the rattling of a coach, for the whining of a door; I talk on, in the same posture of praying; . . . and if God . . . should ask me when I thought last of God in that prayer, I cannot tell: sometimes I find that I had forgot what I was about, but when I began to forget it, I cannot tell. A memory of yesterday's pleasures, a fear of tomorrow's dangers, a straw under my knee, a noise in my ear, a light in my eye, an any thing, a nothing, a fancy, a chimera in my brain, troubles me in my prayer.

I derive comfort from this description of such common, yet

persistently effective interruptions to my attempts to pray. A sharp focus in prayer is difficult to maintain. In former times this difficulty in praying was interpreted as the work of the devil; how nice to have an external excuse! It is, perhaps, more a matter of my devotion to the mundane, my concerns for the personal, and my inadequate training and practice. Prayer requires fortitude and dedication to learning about the self. Because we are so capable of self-deception, prayer is one of the few ways in which we find out who we are. Hamlet's uncle, Claudius, has it right: "My words fly up, my thoughts remain below: Words without thoughts never to heaven go" (III.iii.97). Self-knowledge provided by the insights gained in prayer is disconcerting, yet it opens the door to spiritual growth and maturation.

The experience of personal prayer can include a feeling of desperation that occurs when we are not able to pray. There are those moments when prayer seems impossible. The priest in Georges Bernanos' novel, *The Diary of a Country Priest* (1937), writes, "Never have I made such efforts to pray, at first calmly and steadily, then with a kind of savage, concentrated violence, . . . I persisted, almost desperately in a sheer transport of will which set me shuddering with anguish. Yet — nothing." The priest goes on to note that, "the wish to pray is a prayer in itself, that God can ask no more than that of us." This idea is closely allied with accounts in the synoptic gospels that describe Jesus' experiences with prayer. For Jesus, prayer is a personal act, done alone, and probably in silence. In fact, His instructions for prayer in the gospel of Matthew that precede what we call the Lord's Prayer are specific:

". . . go into your room and shut the door and pray to your Father who is in secret, and your Father who sees in secret will reward you. When you are praying, do not heap up empty phrases as the Gentiles do, for they think they will be heard because of their many words. Do not be like them, for your Father knows what you need before you ask him" (Matthew 6:6–8).

The Power of Prayer

For me, prayer is a private affair. It is a demanding mental and spiritual exercise that forces me to attend to my life at the very moment of my prayer. And my prayers are frequent and brief. As Mother Teresa cautions in her book, *No Greater Love* (1997),

Let us free our minds. Let's not pray long, drawn-out prayers, but let's pray short ones full of love. . . . Prayer that comes from the mind and heart is called mental prayer. . . . It is only by mental prayer and spiritual reading that we can cultivate the gift of prayer. . . . In vocal prayer we speak to God; in mental prayer He speaks to us.

Prayer empowers me in several ways essential to my daily life:

1. Prayer is a source of courage in my never-ending struggle to live a virtuous life. Prayer is a process that continually realigns me with the values that define my concept of an honorable life lived under the shadow of the source of all value — God. When the ever-present seven deadly sins become apparent, yet again, it is prayer that can redirect my journey. The companion to courage is, of course, compassion, that feeling toward others that provides the impetus, and gives the strength, to do what must be done. Compassion is a direct gift from God through prayer. My prayers are answered, in part, by the process of praying, which requires that I clarify and define my needs and recall, again, my sources of help.

2. Prayer affirms the significance of all living beings, in particular the value beyond calculation of those, unknown to me, who

suffer. In my self-centered life I must be reminded, again and again through prayer, to hold to the certain knowledge that my privileged existence is not my due, but a factor of chance. My prayers focus my sight on the work that I can and must do today as witness to my faith.

3. Prayer is a process by which I review who I am, and what I have, what I do. This process confirms for me, in the several times a day that I pray, that all I am and have — all that defines me to myself and to others — is a gift of God. My loves, my family and friends, my work, my health, and my material goods are not of my doing. Whatever has been accomplished has been done with and through the gifts given to me of intellect, health, social position, and hope. I could have been the starving baby in the Sudan, the infant thrown into the fire at Auschwitz, or the Spartan infant put out to die. But I am not, and I must take full account of my responsibilities to do what I can with what I have for the God I worship. For, as Paul wrote to the church at Corinth, "God chose the weak in the world to shame the strong; God chose what is low and despised in the world, things that are not, to reduce to nothing things that are . . ." (I Corinthians 1:27–8). I am reminded, in prayer, of my shame.

4. Prayer is a time of awakening. I, often with a smile, realize that an answer, a question, a promise, a demand, a plea, or a denial present within my unconscious will become obvious to me in my times of praying. Often I am not even sure why I am praying at this moment and not another. But openness to hearing the answer allows that answer to come. Much of the significance of my prayers lies in my awakening to what is already happening around me. Coincidences, or Jungian synchronicities, are important because they provide clues to the answers to our prayers. These answers are usually already present in our mental and spiritual lives. We need to be open to seeing and hearing these "judgings"

from the Spirit that push us toward awareness of who we are and what we are to do and be. As the ancient motto of the Benedictine Order states, "To pray is to work, to work is to pray."

THE GOOD WORD

In a universe beyond our comprehension we open our hearts and minds to what we call the Creator and Sustainer of all, hoping against hope that we shall find guidance in our search for a life of value. Brief as we know it to be, we want that life to have meaning, to be defined by virtue, and to have been — in that final analysis — worth living. Whatever means we use to fulfill our yearning, it will be a form of prayer, voiced or not. We need a God worthy of the depth of our prayers, a God who will, finally, through our laying bare our very souls, lead us to peace through our courage and our confidence. Elizabeth Barrett Browning assures us in "Aurora Leigh":

> God answers sharp and sudden on some prayers,
> And thrusts the thing we have prayed for in our face,
> A gauntlet with a gift in't. Every wish
> Is like a prayer . . . with God.

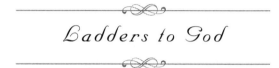

Ladders to God

MARIANNE WILLIAMSON

*P*rayer reweaves the rent fabric of the universe. It releases us, in time, from the snares of lower energies. Total dependence on God makes us independent of the darkness of the world. No problem is too big or small, no question too big or small, no question too important or unimportant to place in His hands. We don't ask God for too much; in fact, we ask for too little. Turn to Him for everything. Give everything to God. The mistake many people make is that although they *believe* in Him, they do not intimately include Him in their lives.

Prayer and meditation reconnect us with our Source. We have gradually become so disassociated from nature, including our own inner nature, that we tend to perceive ourselves as separate from our own ground of being. Spirit is the essence of who we are, the divine energy that permeates all life. To defer to God, to appeal to Him is to humble our mortal, limited selves before the force of consciousness at the center of all things.

And so we embark upon the ways of a prayerful life. Prayer is where we talk to God, stake claim to His thought forms and honor His power to heal us. Prayerful ways are not always easy, for our resistance is great. We have been deluded by the thinking of an arrogant world. Prayer roots us in a different center of emotional gravity. It represents a true conversion from sourcing power in one place to sourcing it in another. It is the spiritualization of our mental habits and the disciplining of our scattered minds. That is why it gives us so much strength.

Prayers increases our faith in the power of good and thus our power to invoke it. Most of us have more faith in the power of AIDS to kill us than we have faith in God to heal us and make us whole. We have more faith in the power of violence to destroy us than we have faith in the power of love to restore us. Where we place our faith, there we will find our treasure. Whatever we choose to look at, we will see. Prayer is a way of focusing our eyes.

Our goal is to bring our lives to prayer. Emotionally, there are no small issues. Anything has the power to hurt, if our mind is vicious enough to use it against us. A torn shirt can drive us to tears, if it reminds us enough of a day in third grade when we felt like our clothes weren't adequate. A small, careless word from someone can trigger a torrent of painful feelings. It is these small, insidious moments of pain that God can cast out but that we alone cannot. Hurt children, their wounds unhealed, too often become very dangerous adults.

We spiritually reconstitute our lives by asking Him to enter us. We invite Him into every situation, to alchemize our thoughts and emotions, to change dramatically our orientation. The ways of prayerfulness are a modulation up from a mode of despair to a mode of hope. A desperate outlook is a choice we make. Peace is simply another one.

Our prayer is for our hearts to stretch to the point of total openness, to radical acceptance and love of others. The path of the pilgrim is the path to a heart that expands and does not constrict. That doesn't mean we won't have sorrowful days, but if there is sorrow, we want sorrow that matters. Both sorrow and joy can stretch us and hone us. The issue is not whether our day is easy, but whether we spend it with an open heart. We use prayer to redesign our lives. We use it to get our minds, and therefore our lives, back on track. After that, we use it to stay there.

"Dear God, please handle this or that" is a prayer for perfection. It means, Please infuse my contribution to this situation with Your wisdom and Your power. Shed Your light. If there is a lack of perfect unfoldment here, I want whatever blocks in my mind that contribute to this problem to be revealed to me and removed. Deliver all darkness to the nothingness from whence it came.

With this attitudinal shift, we change the paradigm that now rules the world. Just as we used to think that the earth was the center of external power and then found out that the sun is, we have been thinking that man's ego is the center of internal power and, at last, we're remembering that God is.

Of course this is blasphemy to the ego; it robs it of its power. But the ego has never given us anything but the illusion of power in our lives. Our choice is to be slaves to the ego, or actualized children of God. God shares His power with us to the extent to which we acknowledge Him as Source. That is not because *He* has an ego, by the way; it is because without that conscious acknowledgment the subconscious mind remains confused about which master it is supposed to serve. Prayer programs divine guidance into the mental computer. It is not an abdication of personal responsibility but rather a profound *taking* of responsibility, the ultimate step toward our full divine empowerment on earth.

Ancient wisdom, then, is modern wisdom.

Humanity's fall from grace means humanity's predilection for thinking the meanest, most fearful, least loving thoughts. The thoughts of God are the thoughts of the Most High, while the thoughts of the fallen human race are thoughts most low. Paradise is the realm of higher thought, and prayer is our ladder back up there.

Prayer is something *we do*. To say a prayer is more than just to think about God. A prayerful attitude is powerful, but the actual utterance of a prayer, silently or aloud, increases the subconscious power of communion with God. In this sense, prayer is God's greatest gift to us, for it is the key to His house.

I once read in an essay on Buddhism that "nothing is so fragile as action without prayer." Prayer aligns our internal energies with truth in a way that mere action cannot. Events ultimately unfold according to subconscious rather than conscious programming, and prayer is a way of healing and releasing the subconscious mind. When we pray that God take a situation into His hands, we are praying for two things: one, that events unfold at the highest vibration of love for all human beings touched in any way by the situation, now and forever; and two, that our minds remain aligned with truth.

If things go well, we pray that we not be tempted to get cocky, proud, or to take success for granted. If things do not go well, we pray that we not be tempted to think the jury is ever in until we see God smiling. It is only giving in to defeat that ultimately brings defeat. Initial rejection or disappointment does not mean God is saying no. It means we're being given the opportunity to see past a crucifixion and to attitudinally invoke resurrection.

Prayer gives us strength to endure, the tools to make miracles.

A few years ago, I was visiting my friend Rose, who found that her daughter was not at a friend's home, where we thought she was. Upon further investigation, we found that not only was she not there, but in fact none of her friends had seen her since ten o'clock the night before. As Rose called every place she could think of to locate her daughter, her panic understandably began to mount. I tried to be helpful but as the list of possibilities narrowed, I too became scared for her daughter's safety. Rose took a Valium to help her relax.

After about twenty minutes, when no further options presented themselves, I said, "Let's say a prayer." We did. Soon after, Rose looked up at me, a deep serenity on her face, and said, "Oh good, the Valium just kicked in." As the irony of what she had just said dawned on her, we burst into our first big laugh of the day. Then her daughter called, safe and sound. Boy is Valium powerful. . . .

My friend was delivered from hell not by the power of drugs but by the power of heaven. The interrelationship between the two states is the meaning of our existence. The physical symbols of both Judaism and Christianity — the Star of David and the cross — represent the right relationship between Heaven and earth, the axis of God intercepting the axis of humanity: As it is above, so shall it be below. To look to God means to look to the realm of consciousness that can deliver us from the pain of living.

The purpose of prayer is to bring Heaven and earth together. It gives inner peace in ways that neither intellectual understanding, credentials, money, sex, drugs, houses, clothes, nor any other gifts of the world can do. We can learn to speak to God as we would speak to a combination therapist/lover/teacher/best-friend/One-we-trust-more-than-anything/One-who-loves-us-no-matter-what/One-with-all-the-power-to-heal/One-with-the-power-and-desire-to-help, for that's what God is. Prayer work is a constant and consistent conversation with Him. God listens, and He answers. His answer is always peace.

Prayer gives us access to a sweeter, more abundant life. The intellect gives many things, but ultimately it cannot give comfort. No conventional therapy can release us from a deep and abiding psychic pain. Through prayer we find what we cannot find elsewhere: a peace that is not of this world.

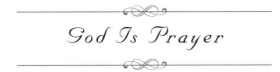

God Is Prayer

MAURICE FRIEDMAN

*T*he Hasidic rebbe Menahem Mendel of Kotzk interpreted the biblical injunction to be holy as meaning "Be humanly holy." Prayer, as much as anything we do, is our way of becoming humanly holy.

"God is of no importance unless He is of supreme importance," wrote the great American Jewish theologian Abraham Joshua Heschel. Praying, therefore, is not the road to enriching the self in either a material or a spiritual sense; for the relationship to God is not a means to our ends. "Prayer may not save us," wrote Heschel, "but prayer makes us worth saving." I was first introduced to Heschel's writings when I read his beautiful essay entitled "Prayer," which he gave to me in mimeographed form long before its publication. In the essay, Heschel defines prayer as "an invitation to God to intervene in our lives" and "a perpetual inner attitude . . . the orientation of human inwardness toward the holy."

Martin Buber, the great Jewish philosopher, defines prayer as "that speech of man to God which, whatever else is asked, ultimately asks for the manifestation of the divine Presence, for this Presence's becoming dialogically perceivable." The simple presupposition of genuine prayer, according to Buber, is "readiness of the whole person for this Presence, simple turned-towardness, unreserved spontaneity": "He who is not present perceives no Presence." The special problem of prayer for the contemporary person is the feeling of self-consciousness or awareness that I am praying. It is this self-conscious awareness that takes away the spontaneity and interferes with this person's relationship of trust. The Hasidim, the Eastern European Jewish mystics of the eighteenth and nineteenth centuries, knew about this same problem of self-consciousness during prayer. Weeping according to plan or thoughts about prayer are both like "alien thoughts" that hinder the soul from fixing itself wholly upon God. One Hasidic rebbe interpreted the biblical injunction against building an altar of hewn stone as a warning against the lack of spontaneity in prayer. "If you do make an altar of words, do not hew and chisel them, for such artifice would profane it."

My own definition of prayer is very simple and owes much to my two teachers and friends, Abraham Joshua Heschel and Martin Buber. Prayer, to me, is an attitude of openness to both the wonder and the claim of existence. "Alas, the world is full of enormous lights and mysteries," said the Baal Shem Tov, the founder of Hasidism, "But man hides them from him[self] with one small hand." Prayer is the removal of that hand. Prayer has to do with discovering anew in each time and situation what we can bring and the way we bring ourselves to a life crisis, a poem, a dream, or a Hasidic, Zen, or Sufi tale. Close to a half century ago, when I had finished my doctoral dissertation on Buber, my chief advisor amazed me by asking, "Do you know Buber's secret? It is prayer." He did not mean that Buber spent so many hours a day praying, but that he brought himself into every hour of his life in a state of real openness. This is what I think my former student and friend Silvio Fittipaldi means in his beautiful little book, *How to Pray Always Without Always Praying* (1978). This life of prayer can only be sustained if we bring ourselves to each situation with all we know and have been. The hosemaker who prayed the Psalms as he worked will be the cornerstone of the Temple until the Messiah comes, said the Baal Shem.

Prayer is not simple. It is personal and communal. It is prescribed liturgy and silent meditation. What Heschel says of Jewish prayer is perhaps true of all great prayer, namely that it is guided by the polar-opposite principles of "order and outburst, regularity and spontaneity, uniformity and individuality, law and freedom, a duty and a prerogative, empathy and self-expression, insight and sensitivity, creed and faith, the word and that which is beyond words." We all have our periods of quiet personal prayer reciting the Psalms, turning silently and humbly to personal dialogue with God. Yet even when we pray alone we are also praying for our family, for our community, for mankind, and for the redemption of the exiled Presence of God and the reuniting of God and the world.

Before praying, a person should prepare to die, taught the Baal Shem, because the intention of praying demands the staking of one's entire self. When the Baal Shem prayed, he often trembled. Once, what was usually just a slight quiver running through his body became a violent shaking and trembling; his face was burning like a torch, and his eyes were wide open and staring like those of a dying man. Once, a disciple smoothed out his robe, and the disciple began to tremble too, and so did the table that the disciple held onto to steady himself. Another time, the water in a nearby trough trembled, and still another time, the grain that filled open barrels nearby trembled.

To many of the zaddikim, the Hasidic rebbes, the true prayer was not for one's own needs, but for the redemption of the Shekinah, God's exiled presence, and the reunion of God and his world. Once Rabbi Barukh of Mezbizh's grandson was playing hide-and-seek with a friend and came crying to his grandfather because his friend ran away and did not try to find him. At this, Rabbi Barukh's eyes brimmed with tears, and he cried, "God says the same thing: 'I hide, but no one wants to seek me.'"

The prayer a person says is, in itself, God, taught Rabbi Pinhas of Koretz. "He who knows that prayer in itself, is God, is like the king's son who takes whatever he needs from the stores of his father." On the first day of the New Year festival, Rabbi Shmelke of Nikolsburg prayed, with tears in his eyes, complaining that the people prayed for nothing but their own needs and did not think of the exile of God's glory. "We pray for the petty needs of the hour," said Rabbi Naftali of Roptchitz, "and do not know how to pray for our redemption." Redemption, for Hasidism as for Judaism in general, does not mean individual salvation but the redemption of the whole of God's creation, the reuniting of God with his exiled Shekinah.

From the Baal Shem Tov onward, the chief characteristic of Hasidic prayer has been to bring one's whole soul and life into prayer. Prayer to the zaddikim, and to Martin Buber, is a dialogue between the worshiper and God. Rabbi Zevi Hirsh of Rymanov taught his disciples that they should sing to God when they rose in the morning and saw that God had returned their souls to them, and he told of a Hasid who, whenever he came to these words in the Morning Prayer, "My God, the soul you have placed in me is pure," danced and broke into a song of praise. One zaddik went further and asserted that one sings unto God in order to bring about that God sings in us!

When a Hasid complained that he did not understand the statement, "I believe with perfect faith" since "If I really do believe, then how can I possibly sin? But if I do not really believe, why am I telling lies?", Rabbi Noah of Lekhovitz explained that the words, "I believe" are really a prayer, meaning, "Oh, that I may believe!" Suffused by a glow from within, the Hasid cried, "That is right! Lord of the Word, oh, that I may believe!" Rabbi Moshe of Kobryn, whenever he came to the words in the seder about the youngest son who does not know how to ask, always paused, sighed, and said to God: "And the one, alas! who does not know how to pray — open his heart so that he may be able to pray." Rabbi Yisakhal Baer of Radoshitz taught that man's prayer is God's prayer; for God not only takes pleasure in the prayer of righteous persons, but wakens those prayers within them and gives them the strength to pray. Rabbi Menahem Mendel of Kotzk (known to the Hasidim as the Kotzker rebbe) advised a Hasid who told him about his poverty and troubles not to worry, but to pray to God with all his heart. When the Hasid replied that he did not know how to pray, pity surged up in the rebbe and he said, "Then you have indeed a great deal to worry about."

Once a Hasid complained to Rabbi Yitzhak Meir of Ger that he had prayed for twenty years, and his praying was no different from when he started. The Rabbi of Ger reminded him of the teaching that one should take the Torah on oneself as the ox takes the yoke. "You see, the ox leaves his stall in the morning, goes to the field, plows, and is led home, and this happens day after day, and nothing changes with regard to the ox, but the plowed fields bear the harvest." The purpose of prayer is not rising to higher spiritual planes, but having a dialogue with God.

"At New Year's," said Rabbi Pinhas, "everyone can see God according to his own nature: one in weeping, one in prayer, and one in the song of praise." Once Rabbi Zusya of Hanipol prayed, "Lord, I love you so much, but I do not fear you enough! Let me stand in awe of you like your angels, who are penetrated by your awe-inspiring name." God answered Zusya's prayer, and his name penetrated Zusya's heart. But Zusya crawled under the bed like a little dog and shook with animal fear, howling, "Lord, let me love you like Zusya again!" And this prayer too was granted.

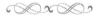

This essay is based on Maurice Friedman's, *A Dialogue with Hasidic Tales: Hallowing the Everyday* (1988), chapter 12.

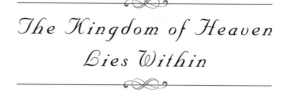

The Kingdom of Heaven Lies Within

ALBERT LOW

Be still,
And know
That I am
God.

MEDITATION AND PRAYER

"The essence of prayer," said Theophan the Recluse, "is lifting the heart towards God." *The Diamond Sutra* (1935) says that we must "Arouse the mind without resting it upon anything." Theophan was a Russian priest who was born in central Russia at the beginning of the nineteenth century and died at its end. Later in life he became a monk in a small monastery and devoted his life to prayer and study and was considered to be the epitome of what is best in Russian Orthodoxy. *The Diamond Sutra,* a scripture of the Mahayana and much beloved of the Zen sect, was written about the fourth century A.D. The above two sayings are strikingly similar. One might say that this is simply an accident of language, but my feeling is that they flow from a common source. I will give a few indicators of why I say this.

First, let's take a look at the word "Zen." It comes from the Sanskrit word, *dhyana,* which means "meditation" — "samadhi" and "going beyond the opposites." Thus Zen is about practice; it is not a philosophy. The practice is called *zazen,* or *sitting* Zen. The highest form of zazen is *shikantaza,* or just sitting. Zazen could be said to be, at its best, *sitting in the presence.* Its purpose is to just be still and know. For Theophan, prayer was "standing before God," or standing in God's presence. Is this then the difference between zazen and prayer: that prayer requires God and zazen does not? When Buddha was asked about a Supreme Being he refused to answer, saying that the question had no bearing on practice; for Theophan, on the other hand, God was essential. Are zazen and prayer quite different, like chalk and cheese?

WHY DO WE PRAY?

Why do we pray? Why do we meditate? It was William James, I believe, who said that the spiritual life begins with the cry for help. In the first few lines of the Twenty-second Psalm one hears the cry:

My God, my God, why hast thou forsaken me?

Why art thou so far from helping me and from the words of my roaring?

O my God, I cry in the daytime, but thou answerest not:

And in this night season, and am not silent.

This was also the cry of Jesus on the cross. It is our own cry, too, when we wake up at night and look down the throat of the abyss of nothing, shudder and draw back in terror.

Buddha was the son of a prince and grew up in a very sheltered environment. He married and had a son, but became very restless and left the protection of the chateau, in which he was living, to visit a nearby town. On the way he met a sick man. Because his life had, until then, been so sheltered, he had not encountered sickness. He was stunned when he asked his charioteer what was wrong with the man who was tottering along the road, and was told, "He is sick, my Lord. All human beings fall victim to sickness in their lives." Buddha was so upset that he rushed back to the chateau. Later, when the memory of this meeting had faded, he left the grounds, again to visit the town. On the way this time he met an old man. Again he was shattered to learn that all people grow old. Again he went back to the protection of the walls of the chateau. On his third try to visit to the town he encountered a dead man. This time the shock was overwhelming.

These three encounters are famous in Buddhism. However, all of us have these encounters, not necessarily in a physical way, but all of us, at some level or another, come to realize our utter vulnerability. Sickness, old age, and death are always stalking us. It is when we find ourselves staring this truth in the face, unable to turn away, that we cry out for help in our helplessness.

Buddha had a fourth encounter. This time he met a monk; he was so impressed by the monk's serenity and peace that he vowed to follow the path leading to emancipation. The monk represents that to which we cry out: Wholeness, Unity, God, Buddha, Allah, Brahman, the names may differ, but the cry is the same. We are driven by pain and suffering, we are called by the possibility of a peace beyond understanding.

Prayer comes from this cry; it is the continuation of this cry. Theophan says, "The Spirit, always present and pleading in us, prays with groanings that cannot be uttered." Christ tells us in the Beatitudes, "Blessed are they that hunger and thirst after righteousness." This cry from the heart, in response to the call, becomes a hunger and a thirst. In Zen this hunger and thirst is called the doubt sensation, but this doubt is not a philosophical or intellectual one. It is likened to having swallowed a red-hot iron ball that one cannot swallow nor cough up. Shibayama, a contemporary Zen master, said of the doubt sensation, "You who have not spent sleepless nights in suffering and tears, who do not know the experience of being unable to swallow even a piece of bread — the grace of God will never reach you."

If the call is loud enough, eventually this hunger will become a constant accompaniment in one's life; prayer then becomes continuous.

UNCEASING PRAYER

If we quote Theophan on prayer fully, he says, "The principal thing is to stand with the mind in the heart before God, and to go on standing before him unceasingly day and night, until the end of life." However, unceasing prayer is a feature not only of the prayers of Theophan, but of Zen as well. The great Zen master Hakuin says, "Walking, standing, sitting, lying down, active, or silent, whether in favorable or unfavorable situations, throw your mind into the question." Ta Hui, another Zen master put it this way, "Whether you are happy or angry, in high or lowly surroundings, drinking tea or eating dinner, at home with your family, meeting guests, on duty at the office, attending a party or celebration, you should always be active and alert and mindful of the Work." How similar this is to Theophan who says, "Let no one think, my fellow Christians, that only priests and monks need pray without ceasing, and not laymen. No, no: Every Christian without exception ought to dwell always in prayer. . . . When we are engaged in manual labor and when we walk or sit down, when we eat or when we drink, we can always pray inwardly."

PRELEST AND MAKYO

One of the most dramatic sayings from the Zen tradition is Zen master Rinzai's, "If you meet the Buddha, kill the Buddha!" An angel of light appeared to one of the Desert Fathers. The apparition said, "I am the angel of Gabriel, and I have been sent to thee." But the father said, "Think again — you must have been sent to somebody else. I haven't done anything to deserve an angel." Immediately the apparition disappeared. One of the big misunderstandings about prayer is that it should lead to visions, ecstasies, highs, and so on. Many people feel that the aim of prayer and meditation is to feel good about themselves. Zen masters warn constantly against this search for experiences, calling them makyo. One finds the same warnings with the Desert Fathers who used the term *prelest*. This means, literally, "wandering" or "going astray." Makyo and prelest both refer to those experiences and visions that occur during prayer, and to which people can become attached. Yasutani Roshi said on one occasion that to see a beautiful vision of an angel does not mean that you are any nearer to becoming one with yourself, anymore than having a dream of being a millionaire means that you are any richer when you awake. Theophan was more scathing in his attack when he said, "Illusion never unites a man who is divided by sin, it does not stop the upsurge of blood, does not lead to repentance . . . it fires the imagination, encourages the rush of blood, brings one a certain tasteless, poisonous enjoyment, and flatters one insidiously, inspiring one with self-conceit and establishing in the soul an idol — 'I.'" Far from seeking visions and ecstasies, the Desert Fathers would say that we should pray "without any image, any process of reasoning, any perceptible movement of thought."

THE GREAT WORK

Another misunderstanding is the belief that prayer and

meditation should be effortless, without difficulty or striving. In reply to this, the Desert Fathers would say, "Complete serenity is a gift of God; but this serenity is not given without our own intense effort. You will achieve nothing by your own efforts alone; yet God will not give you anything, unless you work with all your strength." Bodhidharma, who was the first patriarch of Zen, said that truth could be "attained only by long diligence in a practice difficult to practice and long endurance of that which it is difficult to endure." Zen master Mumom said that one must involve one's three hundred and sixty bones and eighty-four thousand pores in the practice. For the Desert Fathers prayer required "patience, labor, and sweat." Theophan said, "Every struggle in the soul's training, whether physical or mental, that is not accompanied by suffering, that does not require the utmost effort, will bear no fruit. . . . Many people have worked and continue to work without pain, but because of its absence they are strangers to purity and out of communion with the Holy Spirit, because they have turned aside from the severity of suffering."

The Great Gobi Desert

Even those who do not seek visions, who recognize the need for intense effort, may nevertheless become completely discouraged when faced with the desert of the self. As we meditate, or pray, so gradually what we had previously valued and considered essential, may become distasteful. Our sense of our own value and importance is worn down and we seem to enter a lunar landscape of the soul. Those who practice Zen may attend retreats or *sesshins,* and this Great Gobi desert of the soul is then often revealed to them. There they journey in the dust, dry and parched. As Theophan says, "This is a depressing state, but it must be endured with the thought that we do not deserve anything better, that we have earned it. There are no remedies against it, and deliverance depends upon God's will. All we can do is to cry to the Lord: Thy will be done! Have mercy! Help me! But on no account should we allow ourselves to grow slack, for this is harmful and destructive. The Holy Fathers describe such states as cooling off or dryness; and they agree in regarding them as something inevitable for anyone trying to live according to God's will, for without them we quickly become presumptuous."

THE HEART AND HARA

One of the things that the Desert Fathers insist upon is that attention must be held within the heart: "When we strive with diligent sobriety to keep watch over our rational faculties, to control and correct them, how else can we succeed in this task except by collecting our mind, which is dispersed abroad through the senses, and bringing it back into the world within, into the heart itself, which is the storehouse of all our thoughts." On another occasion Theophan said, "Descend from the head into the heart. Then you will see all thoughts clearly, as they move before the eyes of your sharp-sighted mind. But until you descend into the heart, do not expect to have due discrimination of thoughts."

What is the "heart" that plays such an important part in prayer? Most of us associate the heart with the emotions, passions. But in the Bible, and in the teachings of the Orthodox Church, the word had a much wider meaning. One commentator put it thus, "It is the primary organ of man's being, whether physical or spiritual; it is the center of life, the determining principle of all our activities and aspirations." In this way the heart would not simply embrace emotions and affections, but would also embrace the whole of what we would call the person.

In Zen we find an almost identical "center." It is called the *hara,* or more specifically, the *tanden.* The hara is the center of gravity of the whole person. It is the source of a spiritual and psychological energy called *ki* energy or *joriki.* It too is the center of life and the determining principle of all our actions. Development of hara, and therefore the generation of joriki, is essential in the martial arts, in the tea ceremony, and in sumei painting. But it is also essential in the practice of zazen.

GOD AND BUDDHA NATURE

So many more parallels could be drawn between prayer and Zen meditation, but, alas, space does not permit us to draw them. But are prayer and zazen just parallels? Do they never converge? Does prayer take us to God while zazen takes us nowhere? Remembrance of God in prayer is, for Theophan, crucial. But what does this mean? He says that remembrance of God is keeping in mind — without any deliberately imposed concept — of some truth. As Christ said, we must know the truth — the truth will set us free, but truth is not a thought, image, or mental construct of any kind. Christ also told us, "The Kingdom of Heaven lies within." A Desert Father says, when praying, "Enter into the treasure-house that lies within you, and so you will see the treasure-house of heaven: for the two are the same, and there is but a single entry to them both." It is with the same inspiration as the Desert Father that a Zen master, when asked by a disciple, "Where is my treasure-house?" replied, "Your question is your treasure-house."

Saint Paul cried out, "Know ye not your own selves, how that Jesus Christ dwells in you?" Echoing this comes the famous saying of Zen master Hakuin, "From the beginning all beings are Buddha!"

All the quotations of Theophan and the Desert Fathers are taken from *The Art of Prayer,* which is an orthodox anthology compiled by Igumen Chariton of Valamo, translated by E. Kadloubovsky and E. M. Palmer, and edited with an introduction by Timothy Ware (1966).

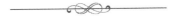

CHAPTER TWO

The Gift of Prayer

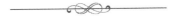

More things are wrought by prayer
Than this world dreams of.

— ALFRED, LORD TENNYSON

The Paradox of Prayer

HENRI J. M. NOUWEN

*T*he paradox of prayer is that we have to learn how to pray yet we can only receive prayer as a gift. It is exactly this paradox that explains why prayer is the subject of so many seemingly contrasting statements.

All the great saints in history and all the spiritual directors worth their salt say that we have to learn to pray, since prayer is our first obligation as well as our highest calling. Many books have been written about the question of how to pray. Many men and women have tried to articulate the different forms and levels of their impressive experiences of prayer, and have encouraged their readers to follow their road. They remind us repeatedly of Paul's words: "Pray constantly" (1 Thessalonians 5:17), and often give elaborate instructions on how to develop an intimate relationship with God. We even find different "schools of prayer," and, not surprisingly, elaborate arguments in favor of one school or another.

One such school or tradition is Hesychasm (from the Greek word *hesychia* meaning "repose"). Theophan the Recluse, a nineteenth-century Russian Hesychast, offers a beautiful example of an instruction in prayer when he writes in *The Art of Prayer* (1966):

> Make yourself a rule always to be with the Lord, keeping your mind in your heart and do not let your thoughts wander; as often as they stray, turn them back again and keep them at home in the closet of your heart and delight in converse with the Lord.

There is no doubt that Theophan, and with him all great spiritual writers, considers serious discipline essential to arriving at an intimate relationship with God. For them, prayer requires continuous and arduous effort. In fact, some spiritual writers have documented their efforts to pray in such concrete and vivid detail that they often leave the reader with the erroneous impression that he or she can reach any level of prayer just by hard work and stern perseverance. This impression has disillusioned many dedicated people who, after long years of strenuous "prayer work," feel they were farther away from God than when they started.

But the same saints and spiritual guides, who speak about the discipline of prayer, also keep reminding us that prayer is a gift of God. They say that we cannot truly pray by ourselves, but that it is God's spirit who prays in us. Paul put it very clearly: "No one can say, 'Jesus is Lord' unless he is under the influence of the Holy Spirit" (1 Corinthians 12:3). We cannot force God into a relationship. God comes to us on His own initiative, and no discipline, effort, or ascetic practice can make Him come. All mystics stress with an impressive unanimity that prayer is "grace"; that is, a free gift from God, to which we can only respond with gratitude.

But they hasten to add that this precious gift indeed is within our reach. In Jesus Christ, God has entered into our lives in the most intimate way, so that we can enter into His life through the Spirit. That is the meaning of the powerful words Jesus spoke to His apostles on the evening before His death: "I must tell you the truth: it is for your own good that I am going because unless I go, the Advocate [that is, the Spirit] will not come to you; but if I do go, I will send him to you" (John 16:7). In Jesus, God became one of us to lead us, through Jesus, into the intimacy of His divine life. Jesus came to us to become as we are and left us to allow us to become as He is. By giving us His Spirit, His breath, Jesus became closer to us than we are to ourselves. It is through our bond with Jesus that we can call God "Abba, Father" and can become part of the mysterious divine relationship between Father and Son. Praying in the Spirit of Jesus Christ, therefore, means participating in the intimate life of God himself.

In *New Seeds of Contemplation* (1961) Thomas Merton writes:

> The union of the Christian with Christ . . . is a mystical union in which Christ Himself becomes the source and principle of life in me. Christ Himself . . . "breathes" in me divinely in giving me His Spirit.

The image that best expresses the intimacy we share with God during prayer is the image of God's breath. We are like asthmatic people who are cured of their anxiety. The Spirit takes away our narrowness (the Latin word for "anxiety" is *angustia* meaning "narrowness") and makes everything new for us. We receive a new breath, a new freedom, and a new life. This new life is the divine life of God Himself. Prayer, therefore, is God's breathing in us, which allows us to become part of the intimacy of God's inner life and be born anew.

So, the paradox of prayer is that it asks for a serious effort while it can only be received as a gift. We cannot plan, organize, or manipulate God, but without a careful discipline, we cannot receive Him either. This paradox of prayer forces us to look beyond the limits of our mortal existence. To the degree that we have been able to dispel our illusion of immortality and have come to the full realization of our fragile mortal condition, we can reach out in freedom to the Creator and Recreator of life and respond to His gifts with gratitude.

Prayer is often considered a weakness, a support system, that is used when we can no longer help ourselves. But this is only true when the God of our prayers is created in our own image and adapted to our own needs and concerns. When, however, prayer makes us reach out to God, not on our own but on His terms, then prayer pulls us away from self-preoccupations, encourages us to leave familiar ground, and challenges us to enter into a new world, which cannot be contained within the narrow boundaries of our minds or hearts. Prayer, therefore, is a great adventure because we enter into a new relationship with a God who is greater than we are and defies all our calculations and predictions. The movement from illusion to prayer is hard to make since it leads us from false certainties to true uncertainties, from an easy support system to a risky surrender, and from the many "safe" gods to the God whose love has no limits.

Say Yes to God's
Gift of Prayer

DALE EVANS ROGERS

The paradox of prayer is that we have to learn
how to pray yet we can only receive it as a gift.
— HENRI J. M. NOUWEN

Our Father, who has set a restlessness in our hearts and made
us all seekers after that which we can never fully find . . .
keep us at tasks too hard for us,
that we may be driven to Thee for strength.
— A PRAYER ELEANOR ROOSEVELT CARRIED IN HER PURSE

*T*he year was 1962. The setting was Rice University Stadium in Houston, Texas. The event was the citywide Billy Graham Crusade. The audience was made up of 45,000 attentive and eager listeners.

I was sitting on the platform with tears in my eyes. Roy, my husband, was at the podium, speaking. It was Roy's first witness to a crowd of this size.

"Dale worked with God to bring me something I had longed for all of my life — peace. Materially speaking, for years I had nothing. Then for years I had much. But I soon learned that having too much is worse than having too little. Nothing ever seemed quite right. I was restless, confused, unsatisfied. But then I learned that the power of prayer and the feeling of spiritual blessedness and the love of Jesus have no price tags," said Roy.

The stadium was locked in a dead silence. It seemed that all of the 45,000 people were holding their breath for what would come next. Roy went on to describe the strength he gained through daily prayer and reflective Bible reading. Then he closed his witness by denying the published rumors that he was thinking of leaving show business and becoming an evangelist. "If I was going to be an evangelist," he said smiling, "I guess I'd have to do it on horseback, because being a cowboy is all I know." And as Roy's smile gave way to a wide boyish grin, the crowd melted and broke out with thunderous applause.

Yes, God's gift of prayer has been a powerful sustaining force in our home for many years — through difficult times as well as in good times. And this we know for sure, prayer — agonizing prayer — saw both of us through the two years that we cared for our little Robin, our Down's Syndrome baby, our "angel unaware." When she left us to be with her heavenly Father, it was prayer that kept us steady. It was prayer, ours and those of our friends, that saw us through the tragic deaths of our daughter Debbie on the church bus and our son Sandy in Germany.

In all of this we've been reminded over and over again of the definition of prayer given us by one of our Bible teachers. She told us that prayer should be: first, praise of God; second, thanksgiving for His love and guidance; and, third, petition for ourselves and our needs. And her final word was, "You can trust Him implicitly for the answer."

How true! Yet there have been those days — yes, weeks and even months — when it seemed that God was strangely silent to my heartaches and hurts. But slowly I've come to understand, just a little bit, the truth behind these thoughts of Henry Ward Beecher, the powerful nineteenth-century preacher, who wrote in his little book entitled *Aids to Prayer*, "Think not that God's silence is coldness or indifference! When Christ stood by the dead, the silence of tears interpreted His sympathy more wonderfully than even that voice which afterwards called back the footsteps of the brother (Lazarus), and planted them in life again. When birds are on the nest, preparing to bring forth life, they never sing."

An unidentified writer made this intriguing comment: "There is no music in a nest, but there is the making of music in it." In the melody of our lives' experiences we often come to those times of silence and "rests." It is important in such moments not to feel that the life melody is over but to look expectantly for the next movement to begin. God is still the divine Conductor.

In our humanness we fall victim so often to the notion that God should act on our schedule and timetable and in ways that we can readily understand. There is an ever-present danger that we may come to see prayer as a form of heavenly room service. We tend to lose sight of the truth that the purpose of prayer is not to change God or to activate Him. Rather the purpose of prayer is to change us. I like the way author Søren Kierkegaard expressed this idea: "Prayer does not change God, but changes him who prays."

Author Henri Nouwen enriches our understanding of prayer in his essay "The Paradox of Prayer" in which he writes, "When . . . prayer makes us reach out to God, not on our own but on His terms, then prayer pulls us away from self-preoccupations, encourages us to leave familiar ground, and challenges us to enter into a new world, which cannot be contained within the narrow boundaries of our minds and hearts." Then Nouwen adds, "Prayer, therefore, is a great adventure because we enter into a new relationship with a God who is greater than we are and defies all calculations and predictions."

Expressing this same line of thought is a comment credited to the late William Temple, the ninety-eighth Archbishop of Canterbury: "When I say my prayers, I find that coincidences begin to happen." On the other hand, it is important that we strive for an understanding of prayer that avoids its misuse. James Houston cautions against this in his perceptive book entitled *The Transforming Friendship* (1989): "It is alarmingly easy for prayer to become a kind of magical device which we use to get our own way."

Our desire to understand the true purpose of prayer leads us, in our Christian pilgrimage, to not only say "Yes" to God's gift of prayer but also to pose the same request that Jesus's disciples put to Him one day. Luke speaks of the incident in these words: "Once, in a certain place, Jesus was at prayer. When he ceased, one of his disciples said, 'Lord, teach us to pray' " (Luke 11:1 NEB).

Jesus' response to this request was simple and uncomplicated, but very much to the point:

Father, may your name be honoured — may your kingdom come! Give us each day the bread we need, and forgive us our sins, for we forgive anyone who owes anything to us; and keep us clear of temptation. (Luke 11:2–4 Phillips)

This has become known as "the Lord's Prayer" and is certainly the supreme model for us of the gift of prayer. While Luke's wording of Jesus' response to His disciples is considerably shorter than the one found in the Gospel of Matthew (see 6:9–13), it gives us everything we need to come to an understanding of how we are to use God's gift of prayer and what we are to pray for.

Space prohibits me from making an exhaustive commentary on the Lord's Prayer, but I want to express a little of what it has come to mean to me. First, Jesus prays, "Father." This was the traditional opening for *any* Jewish prayer. However, in this instance Jesus used a most untraditional Aramaic word for Father — *Abba*. This is the word a child would have used in speaking to a human father. Jesus' use of the Aramaic word for "Father" gives us a sense of intimacy, respect, and reverence that shifts prayer from a ritual to a profoundly personal and intimate experience and relationship — quite the opposite to a flippant or casual approach.

For Jesus, the Father was not a vague, faraway entity but an intimate and nearby Father — one who cares deeply about everything that concerns us. The apostle Paul expressed it this way for those first-century Christians who were struggling with the idea of this kind of God:

> To prove that you are sons, God has sent into our hearts
> The Spirit of his Son, crying "Abba! Father!" You are there-
> fore no longer a slave but a son, and if a son, then also by
> God's own act an heir. (Galatians 4:6 NEB)

Next in the Lord's Prayer, Jesus says, "May your name be honored" or "hallowed be your name." This heavenly Father of ours is also the Creator-God who spoke the universe into existence and is to be revered. In the words of Isaiah the prophet, He is the Holy One. Over the centuries Christian believers have struggled long and hard for a human understanding of God, and in that struggle the temptation to bring Him down to our size often rears its ugly head.

Human experience makes it clear that we will never understand God in this life, but we are to revere all that we do understand Him to be. Augustine put it very succinctly when he said, "If you have understood, then what you have understood is not God."

We get a deeper understanding of what is happening in the Lord's Prayer when we realize that the reference to God's name goes far beyond the way we use the word. To the Jews the word for "name" referred to a person's total character. As William Barclay says in *The Gospel of Luke* (1975), to pray "may your name be honored" means "far more than knowing that God's name is Jehovah. It means that those who know the whole character and mind and heart of God will gladly put their trust in him." And in praying "may your kingdom come," we are asking that God's will may become a reality to Christian believers now and in all of the future.

The writer of the Matthew version of the prayer adds this sentence, "Thy will be done in earth, as it is in heaven" (6:10 KJV). It seems to me that this is the central petition of the Lord's Prayer and needs to be central in all of our praying. Only then can we move on to the remaining petitions of the prayer.

If we look at how prayer is treated in the Book of Acts we see the pattern the early Christians followed under the leadership and teaching of the apostles — their prayers were always for God's will to be done, even as they prayed for others. For them, and for us, prayer is intended to be an intimate part of all of life — not something to be used only when we're in trouble or at eleven o'clock on Sunday morning.

In his books and sermons, Samuel Shoemaker had a most perceptive way of conveying truth. On one occasion he said, "Prayer is not calling in the fire department; prayer is seeking to live so that the house does not get on fire. Prayer is not the 'last resort,' it is the first thought in every situation. . . . Prayer is communion between two 'people' who increasingly know each other. And one of these 'people' is very decidedly a Senior Partner in the relationship" (*And Thy Neighbor*, 1967).

So far, in the Lord's Prayer our attention has been focused on God:

> Our Father in heaven,
> hallowed be your name.
> Your kingdom come.
> Your will be done,
> on earth as it is in heaven. (Matthew 6:9–10)

Now the focus shifts to us and our needs:

> Give us this day our daily bread.
> And forgive us our debts,
> as we also have forgiven our debtors,
> And do not bring us to the time of trial,
> But rescue us from the evil one. (Matthew 6:11–13)

First, Jesus directed our thoughts to God and His will for everyone. Now comes the acknowledgment that this same God is concerned about and equal to our needs here and now; He forgives our sins and wipes out our debts; and, finally, we can look to the future in confidence, knowing that the Father will support us in our times of testing and trial.

Behind all of Jesus' teaching is the truth that the Father is a God of love Who cares intimately for each one of us. Teresa of Avila, a devout sixteenth-century Spanish Christian, captured the true meaning of prayer when she said, "Prayer is not a matter of thinking a great deal but of loving a great deal." In writing to Christians everywhere and in all of time, the writer of the Book of

Jude counseled his readers with these words, "But you, my friends, must fortify yourselves in your most sacred faith. Continue to pray in the power of the Holy Spirit. *Keep yourselves in the love of God*" (1:20–21 NEB, italics mine).

Reflecting on God's gift of prayer to people like us is an awesome experience. In a sermon entitled "The World's Greatest Power: PRAYER," Norman Vincent Peale asks the question, "What is the greatest power in the universe?" In response he adds, "Is it the enormous force of the hurricane, or the tornado, or the tidal wave, or the earthquake, or the exploding volcano?" He then defines this power in these electric phrases: "I believe that it is the mechanism by which man on earth establishes a connection that provides the flow of power between the mighty Creator and Himself, between the great God who scattered the stars in the infinite night sky and the creature made in His own image: man. The flow of power between the Creator and man is the world's greatest power. And it is released and transmitted by means of a mechanism known as prayer" (*PLUS*, 1992). But it is a power that calls for action on our part if it is to be effective.

One of the greatest and most endearing preachers of the past generation was Paul S. Rees. He had the knack of packing profound truth into a few words: "If we are willing to take hours on end to learn to play the piano, or operate a computer, or fly an airplane, it is sheer nonsense for us to imagine that we can learn the high art of getting guidance through communion with the Lord without being willing to set aside time for it. It is no accident that the Bible speaks of prayer as a form of waiting on God" *(Don't Sleep Through the Revolution, 1969).*

In the midst of our busy and hectic lives taking a step toward this *"waiting on God"* may involve putting into practice an idea suggested by Frank Laubach. Picking up on the pray-without-ceasing principle, as expressed by the apostle Paul, Laubach suggested saying instant or quick prayers right in the middle of the hustle and bustle of life: A one-sentence prayer while sitting in the doctor's waiting room, "Lord, bless the doctor and give him wisdom." Or a prayer for Jane after dialing her number and waiting for an answer, "Bless Jane, Lord, as she takes on her responsibilities in her new job." Or while waiting for a bus or a taxi or an airplane, "Oh God, guide the hand of the driver (pilot) and give us a safe trip." Or while sitting prayerfully in your pew at church waiting for the service to begin, "Father, speak to me this morning and help me to be open to You and everyone around me." Or while waiting at a traffic signal for the red light to turn to green, while standing in the grocery checkout line, while walking four laps in the mall, or while walking the dog in the early morning hours — all of these daily routines offer the opportunity for short prayers that can enrich our own lives and the lives of the people we are praying for.

In the early centuries of the Christian church, the Desert Fathers, quite likely in the vicinity of Mount Sinai, put together a very simple ten-word prayer that has become known as "the Jesus Prayer": "Lord Jesus Christ, Son of God, have mercy on me." Throughout the centuries both clergy and lay people have seen in these few words the summation of the Christian faith, and it is used widely by people who pray in all parts of the world as a means of grace and a sustainer of the faith.

An unknown writer left us this gem:

Prayer is so simple;
It is like quietly opening a door and
     slipping into the very presence of
     God.
There in the stillness

To listen to His voice,
>   perhaps to petition,
>   or only to listen.
It matters not,
>   just to be there, in His presence . . .
In prayer.

Another unknown writer left behind these incisive reflections on the Lord's Prayer.

I cannot pray *our,*
>   if my faith has no room for others and their needs.
I cannot pray *Father,*
>   if I do not demonstrate this relationship to God in
>   my daily living.
I cannot pray *who art in heaven,*
>   if all my interests and pursuits are in earthly things.
I cannot pray *hallowed be Thy name,*
>   if I'm not striving with God's help to be holy.
I cannot pray *Thy kingdom come,*
>   if I am unwilling or resentful of having it in my life.
I cannot pray *on earth as it is in heaven,*
>   unless I am truly ready to give myself to God's
>   service here and now.
I cannot pray *give us this day our daily bread,*
>   without expending honest effort for it,
>   or if I would withhold from my neighbor the bread
>   that I receive.
I cannot pray *forgive us our trespasses as we forgive those
>   who trespass against us,*
>   if I continue to harbor a grudge against anyone.
I cannot pray *lead us not into temptation,*

if I deliberately choose to remain in a situation
where I am likely to be tempted.
I cannot pray *deliver us from evil,*
if I am not prepared to fight and resist evil.
I cannot pray *Thine is the kingdom,*
if I am unwilling to obey the King.
I cannot pray *Thine is the power and the glory,*
if I'm seeking power for myself and for my own glory
first.
I cannot pray *forever and ever,*
if I am too anxious about each day's affairs.
I cannot pray *Amen,*
unless I can honestly say,
"Cost what it may, this is my prayer."

Our pastor, the Reverend William Hanson, offered this prayer, which I have taken as my own: "Lord, we confess that we cling to a safe and comfortable faith. We are not looking for challenges, and we do not like to take risks. Forgive us for taming your gospel and reshaping your teachings to our liking. Forgive us, Lord, and help us to break free from the false security of our own comfort to the true security of faith. Change us in such a way that we may become willing to risk our hearts and lives in following and serving you. Amen."

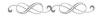

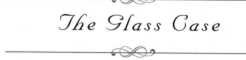

The Glass Case

Frances H. Bachelder

Prayer has greater significance than one can ever know. Even a child, who has not yet learned the true meaning of prayer, often prays with no inkling of its power. When I was about five years old, I asked my father,

"Papa, may I have a penny for some candy squirrel nuts at the store?"

"Sure," he replied, "and since it's you, here are five pennies!"

Remembering the miracle of the five loaves of bread that fed the five thousand, I was delighted that I received not just one penny, but five! A miracle indeed. My simple request had yielded a bounteous blessing in the same way that a bud opens into a beautiful flower with direction and nurturance from a higher source.

As I set out for the candy store with the five pennies jingling in my pocket, I thought about what a wonderful father I had. No matter how busy he was, he never hesitated to listen to me. Not that he *always* granted my wishes. If, at times, what I wanted was not good for me, then my desire — my prayer — was denied. And although at that young age I did not fully understand, I now know that my father was wise and so sometimes refused a request because of his love for me.

Within minutes, I reached the store at the end of the street. I opened the door and stepped inside. There, to the left, was a case with a shiny glass front inside of which I could see all kinds of temptations. The owner saw me come in and went directly to the back of the case because I'd been there for candy many times before. Now I had a decision to make: Should I spend the one penny I had asked for, or all five? As I recall, I put my forefinger on the glass and said, "I'd like a penny's worth of those squirrel nut candies, please." The woman slid the case door back, reached in, and, one by one, dropped five pieces of candy into a little white paper bag. She folded the top down, handed the bag to me, and I gave her a penny. She thanked me and I hurried out of the store with the candy and the four remaining pennies.

Did I innocently follow a basic moral tenet, that of resisting temptation? I wonder. No one said not to spend all five pennies. Perhaps unwittingly I had been inspired by my small inner voice, which told me what to do. I do know my choice felt right to me. Now I wish I could remember what I eventually did with those four extra pennies.

The incident, which I can only view through the sometimes blurred lens of childhood memory, must have made a vivid impression on me because I think of it often. Perhaps it was more important than I realized, for, as I look back on it now, I see that a simple prayer was one of my first conscious acts of will.

When I grew older, I thought about the things that were granted me as a child, all of which required little effort on my part. Why then, I wondered, weren't all my prayers answered as readily as had been that request to satisfy my sweet tooth? I was certain that God listened to my prayers, but something was missing. Then one day, it became clear that I should do my part to reach my goals, accomplish difficult tasks, and make weighty decisions. No doubt there are those who would say, "Oh, that's the reverse order," meaning that I should ask for His guidance *first* and not try to act alone. But I have found that, for me, the asking-first method is not satisfactory. After I have done all I can and am still not successful, *then* I ask for guidance. I'm not certain why I use this sequence, except for one thing: To put a situation in His hands without any effort from me gives me an uncomfortable feeling. I need to take responsibility for my actions, to try my best, before I call upon His strength and wisdom. This, I think, is an individual matter and subject to debate. Either way, however, the power of prayer remains.

At this point in writing this essay I struck a snag. For several days I gave much thought to the next section of this piece. I visited the library, consulting book after book, and also delved into resources in our home. At times, I thought I was ready to start again, but each time I sat down at the typewriter, I discovered that I had more research and thinking to do. I discussed my ideas with my family, and finally when I thought I could not continue, I said a prayer. Then one day a thought came to me — not in bits and pieces — but in a flash, whole and fully rendered. I had done my part and God helped me once again. That insight is described in the following true account.

I vividly recall a high school classmate who, while in his junior year, had a spiritual experience that ultimately led to a successful career. At first, school was of no interest or value to him. He attended only because he was too young to leave, so he coasted through his freshman and sophomore years. Although he dreamed of going to college so that he could be on the football team, his lack of motivation to perform well in school made his goal seem highly improbable.

The young man worked afternoons in a grocery store, but in the evenings, instead of studying, he read books about sports and listened to baseball games on the radio. This routine went on for two years, and when he began his junior year, he was unaware of a tremendous change that was about to take place in his life.

On the first day of school, he sat through his morning classes and then went to lunch in the gymnasium where tables were set up. As was the custom in those days, the jukebox was playing dance music. Having finished his lunch, he found a dance partner and they joined the rest of the "jitterbugs" on the gymnasium floor.

When lunch period ended, he made his way to his fifth-period current history class. He slid into a seat, the bell rang, and the chattering stopped. Then it happened. After placing his book on the desk, he looked up and noticed that the teacher was new. For a fraction of a second, he felt like a different student. I still recall his excitement when he told me about the vivid, almost palpable sensation he had. He said, "This teacher knew nothing about me. I was determined to make a fresh start." From then on, he did excellent work, not only in history, but in all his subjects. There was no stopping him. He graduated from high school and went on to college, where he played football for three years and was co-captain during his last year. He earned his masters and doctoral degrees; became assistant to the provost at a nearby university; served as chairman of a committee representing a consortium of eleven major universities, which oversaw the development of cooperative graduate level programs; and finally, at age forty-nine, he became president of a university. His rapid growth and personal development coupled with his desire to do better work was actually a prayer — and God helped him.

Many years later, he told me more of the story. The new teacher was, of course, his main incentive, but his dentist and a school friend also helped motivate him to succeed. His friend encouraged him and steadfastly assured him that he would go to college and also play football. When his dentist asked if he were planning on college and he replied that he was, the dentist then asked, "Are you a good student? If you don't get good grades, you can't get into college."

Whether or not the dentist and his friend interceded with prayers, I don't know. Just coming in contact with them, however, surely helped him to move in the right direction. The belief of other people in his ability to succeed acted like a force, impelling him toward his goal. Apparently, although he was unaware of it, their belief in him influenced him in a subtle but significant way.

Obviously prayer should not always be for our own sake, but for the sake of others, too. If this was not so, why then do we pray for those who are ill, or fearful, or resentful, or facing one of the myriad pains and difficulties that life by its very nature inevitably sends our way? I believe that God intends us to lead our lives in this way: to struggle as best we can against the complexities of living in this world and to turn to Him when we or others need His loving care. If troubles or problems can be lessened or solved by one person's intercessory prayers, then imagine the healing power that one hundred people can generate when praying together for a lost or pain-wracked soul! Helping others should give us a peaceful feeling, not in an egotistical way but in the sense that we are living life as God intended. If we pray for ourselves and He helps us, then it seems to me that the right thing to do is to pray for others so that they may receive the same blessings. Since we are all God's children we are all from the same family, and, like family, we must help and protect one another.

How can anyone realize the power of prayer unless he or she prays? Some began praying formally when they were young, but for some reason may have stopped. Even so, Ralph Waldo Emerson said that "all men are always praying and all prayers are answered." Our very lives are, in a sense, a kind of prayer, a message to God about not only our needs but also our gratitude for His many blessings, both great and small.

For me the process of writing this essay has been a prayer from the beginning. Although I've thanked God every day for His encouragement during this project, I often felt that a simple "thank you" was not enough. Finally I asked myself, "What more can I do to show Him my gratitude?" Finally, an idea occurred to me: What better way could there be than to read the powerful Book of Psalms? Because of my love for music, I was even more convinced that my decision was a good one after reading the following in *A Gift of Music* (1978) by Jane Stuart Smith and Betty Carlson:

> Psalm 121 is an example of a superb union of words and music. It can well be said that [Heinrich] Schütz unlocked the music hidden in the Psalms. He was the greatest composer of Psalm settings in the history of music.

And Carl E. Seashore wrote in *Psychology of Music* (1938):

> Music is the medium through which we express our feelings of joy and sorrow, love . . . penitence and praise. It is the

charm of the soul, the instrument that lifts the mind to higher regions. . . . It causes emotions to pass over our being like waves over the far reaching sea.

Liszt once wrote that "music . . . contains a great power to move and inspire." Was it not God who gave the world's great composers the gift of creating magnificent music?

As I continued to write, I stopped every now and then to read a few Psalms, also known as spiritual songs. I paid special attention to those concerning gratitude, thanksgiving, and glory to God. My ultimate goal was to read all of the Psalms and to explore the melodies and motifs I found there.

I took a hymnal from the bookcase and searched for words taken directly from the Psalms. This led to my playing these hymns on the piano and recalling how I used to accompany the children during Sunday School worship service. I can still hear them singing, and in that singing, I hear God's grace and love.

As yet, no one has discovered why music affects us the way it does. Its power is overwhelming, as is the power of prayer. Could it be that the two are closely related? Perhaps some day the mystery or secret will be revealed.

At the time I was invited to contribute to this book, my sister had just passed away. With my spirits dimmed, I wondered if I could concentrate. I was tempted to refuse; what should I do? After debating the decision for several days, I asked for help, and it was not long before His answer came: "You should accept the challenge, especially now."

Of the essays I've written and published, this one has been the most difficult to write. I know, however, that it's been worth the effort. I called on God many times and He gave me the courage to continue. Slowly — with a sentence here, a paragraph there — the pages accumulated. And so, with my Bible beside me, and a lot of loving help from God and my family, I have finished this essay and have found joy and comfort in doing so. The whole process has been a prayer that supported me through a difficult period. As Verdi once said while composing during a sad time in his life, "Today a verse; tomorrow another; one time a note, another a phrase . . . little by little the opera was done."

Once again I am reminded of the candy case with the glass front in that long-gone little store. I remember my request for a penny that miraculously became five. I see my father's face, shining with love. That childhood incident has guided me in ways I could not foresee, affecting my life in every way by making me aware of my relationship with my Creator.

As Paul wrote in his first letter to the Corinthians (13:13), "Faith, hope, love abide, these three; but the greatest of these is love."

Thank you, God, for being there
And always listening to my prayers.
Please take care of my sister, who
Now in your hands, is there with you.
            Amen.

What Should I Do with My Life?

DREW LEDER, M.D., PH.D.

"Massapequa, Massapequa Park!" The conductor's voice rang out like the voice of God. Riding the Long Island Railroad, I alternately sat and paced the aisle. I was a welter of confusion struggling to coalesce into a decision. Just the small matter of *what should I do with my life?* The question of my career choice, lurking in the background since I was a young boy, had surfaced with painful urgency. I was fast approaching the age of thirty and was about to be cast forth from postgraduate training into that most dreaded thing — "the real world."

Finishing two advanced degrees, one in medicine, the other a Ph.D. in philosophy, I still wasn't clear which career to pursue. In the face of my fears, I felt powerless to act.

Medicine I had come to associate with rigid hierarchies and

raging egos. And that's just speaking of the doctors. Did I really want to deal with the patients, all those sick people and crazies (for within medicine, I inclined toward psychiatry)? Could I handle the awesome responsibilities and stress?

My father had been a highly successful physician. One day he came home early from the office, downed a few drinks, and jumped from our eighth-story window. Perhaps this, too, factored into my paralysis. Might I end up like that? Or might I spend my psychiatric career trying to magically save him, an effort that would be doomed from the start?

But neither could I embrace a career in academics. This seemed like an uncharted sea, especially with the ports of call (tenure-track jobs) so few and far between. And even if I found a job, I'd likely be stuck in some Midwest college town — a lonely exile for this Manhattan-bred boy.

Then, too, I was frozen by that imperative to "Be a doctor!" that I'd been hearing from my parents since I was in the womb (okay, a slight exaggeration). Later on, my mother would joke: "You can decide what to do with your life — *after* you go to medical school." Ironically, this is what I was now attempting, only I couldn't decide.

This incapacity, along with stabbing fear, guilt, and a low-grade depression, led me to a Twelve Step program. Pioneered by Alcoholics Anonymous in the 1930s, this spiritual path has since proved helpful for treating all kinds of obsessive thought and compulsive behavior.

I'd been working on the Second Step: "Came to believe that a Power greater than ourselves could restore us to sanity." Coming from a family of atheists, I had no belief in or direct experience of God. But I knew that only a restoration to sanity — the ability to think clearly and discern right from wrong — could break this mental logjam.

So the prayer of my heart was simple: "Help!" I needed divine guidance and power. I asked repeatedly to know what God would have me do with my life. Unlike many other prayers I have uttered, this one was sincere. I was honestly ready to accept whatever answer came.

"Be a doctor" was the one I most expected. I'd mulled things over for weeks from a spiritual angle, and an emerging direction seemed clear. It was through a career in medicine — not the self-indulgent pleasures of academe — that I could best relieve suffering and even save lives. True, the path would be rigorous. I'd have to overcome a lifelong dislike of medicine. But this was where I could best contribute to God's healing mission for the world.

"Massapequa, Massapequa Park!" The train jerked and swayed through the Long Island flatlands. Then suddenly I was pierced by a thought: *My image of God is based on my parents.* I was imagining God as some cosmic Matriarch who, like my mother, would demand I be a doctor. My mother, I assumed, viewed medicine as a most lucrative, prestigious, and secure career. Here, I could excel. God, I imagined, wanted me to become a doctor that I might excel at service. Not that different. I was feeling that old parental pressure to "be the best," simply dressed up in spiritual finery.

Now what? If God wasn't my parents, who was He or She? I sat feeling blank and empty. What was God's will for me? I had absolutely no idea.

Then an answer pierced my mind. *"I'm to be a college teacher."* The words were clear and unequivocal. Not a doctor. Not even a "university professor" or "philosopher," with their self-aggrandizing tone. A "college teacher."

Why that? *"Because that's what you want to do,"* I heard. *"God's will is nothing other than the deepest wishes of your own heart."*

Like a hammer, these words shattered all my previous images of God. God was not some cosmic Parent imposing his will upon me from outside, albeit "for my own good." God dwelled within the very breath of my soul.

More followed in a rapid litany. My profession now clarified, I was then told how to perform in my new career. I became aware of essential guiding principles through a vowel acronym: A, E, I, O, U. I sensed that "A" stood for "attention" — a deep receptiveness I was to have with my students and the subject we studied. "E" stood for "energy" and "enthusiasm" — perhaps my greatest strengths as a teacher. "I" was for "integrity." Though a people pleaser, I was to operate with courageous integrity on matters of principle. "U" stood for "unselfishness." I was to give of myself freely as a teacher, even when it was hard or inconvenient.

But what to make of the letter "O"? No corresponding virtue came to mind. Then, like a blurred image coming into focus, I saw the answer clearly. In the A-E-I-O-U procession of vowels, "O" is a circle standing between "I" and "U". And this was a symbol of God. He was not only within, but He was the circle that linked "I" (me) and "U" (you); the spiritual connection between self and others. I realized that as long as my career remained spiritually rooted, it would bear fruit.

I saw I could maintain my spiritual focus through working with the Twelve Step program. And if I did so, that inner voice told me, the gifts I might have used as a psychiatrist would not go to waste. I could help others heal, after all, by passing on this life-saving program. And such work would be free of the toxic beliefs that might have poisoned a psychiatric career. I wouldn't pretend I was the healthy one ministering to the sick. I couldn't demand payment for my services. I wouldn't imagine that the recovery of others rested squarely on my shoulders. Such recovery was the free gift of a loving God.

"Stony Brook!" I was home at last. As I climbed down from the train onto the familiar platform, everything seemed wonderfully transformed. I felt like a child on Christmas morning and the world was a huge present, newly unwrapped. The sky was sapphire blue. The clouds raced in the wind like white-sailed schooners. Even the trees were strange and marvelous. The sight of their branches waving in the breeze felt like hands caressing my cheeks. I remember singing "Amazing Grace" — "I once was lost, but now am found. Was blind, but now I see." Yes, yes that's it! I also remember hugging a dog.

Gradually, of course, my awareness of the world's numinosity faded. To a degree, I purposefully shut it out. All those caressing trees became vaguely threatening. I wanted to return to normal.

But the results of that prayer experience (and of many others since) continue to radiate through my life. The sense of a "God within" (rather than a cosmic Matriarch) helped me over a spiritual block. I could pray with newfound trust and security. This has helped my progress in the Twelve Step program, which has been an agent of healing for myself and many others I've had the privilege to work with over the years.

My subsequent career? Not surprisingly, everything worked out for the best. Against great odds, I found a job as a professor (sorry, college teacher) at Loyola College in Maryland. I'm still happily employed there some twelve years later. I've not for a moment had reason to question my choice of career, which has brought me great riches and pleasures. The power of God runs deep.

God's Continuing Gift

SHUMA CHAKRAVARTY

I sometimes think that the stars are God's tears. Even God's sorrow has created sources of great illumination, joy, and beauty through these shining planets. At our very best, we human beings are microcosms, containing within us a spark of divinity. Therefore, I think that my own heart, shattered by recent sorrows, is like a cascade of diamonds. Each piece is valuable and radiant and a source of joy and illumination to beings known and unknown to me, as the stars are a source of strength and radiance to me, although I am unknown to those distant planets.

Prayer is the most powerful resource we have, for it is our fax line to God. The dazzling array and arsenal of human-created technology, enables NASA ground staff, for instance, to converse with astronauts in space. However, only prayer can illumine and ennoble a broken heart or a despairing mind.

What is prayer? There are as many responses to that question as there are people.

Perhaps it is easier to define what prayer is NOT, rather than what it is. Prayer is NOT a recitation of fantasies, cravings, and demands. Prayer is NOT a monologue in an echo chamber. Prayer is NOT ventriloquism nor self-hypnosis. Prayer is NOT a self-convincing day-dream nor is it shadow-boxing in a hall of mirrors.

What then is prayer and WHY is it powerful?

My experience and understanding of prayer is that it is God's continuing gift to Creation. Prayer is our grace-given ability to contact the Creator immediately without intermediary or interruption. Our soul is the divine spark within our flawed and fractured being which remains radiant, unpolluted by our errors, for the SOUL IS OF GOD! Through genuine prayer we can commune with our Creator and find whatever we really need (not necessarily what we erroneously desire) for our sojourn on this narrow bridge of Life.

Why narrow? Life is often beset with difficulties. Life is also of unknown duration; beginning and ending in Mystery. To this mystic, human life is a bamboo bridge between Eternity and Infinity — the unknown polarities which precede birth and succeed death. During the duration of a mortal's life of a handful of decades, prayer is the most powerful gift God has given us to contact our Source — to aid and empower us on this mysterious voyage of Life.

If prayer is our cherished choice then it will NOT be a sporadic S.O.S. but the pulse and cadence of our constant devotion to God. Only through the power of prayer can a being truly become a source of strength and light and loving-kindness to all beings.

Therefore, I aspire to be one of God's fireflies, bringing a spark of radiance and reassurance to fellow-creatures in this amazing adventure from Mystery to Mystery!

CHAPTER THREE

Connecting
with God

*God dwells far from us, but prayer brings
Him down to our earth, and links
His power with our efforts.*

— MADAME DE GASPARIN

The Origins of Prayer
in Children

MARK R. BANSCHICK, M.D.

If one were to essay a minimal definition of religion today
it would perhaps not be Tylor's famous "belief in spiritual beings,"
to which Goody, wearied of theoretical subtleties, has lately urged
us to return, but rather what Salvdor de Madariaga has called
"the relatively modest dogma that God is not mad."

—CLIFFORD GEERTZ, THE INTERPRETATION OF CULTURES (1973)

*I*t does not take much for a child to pray. He opens up his heart and says a few words to a God who cares. No major theological debate is required, no ruminations over the validity of religion. When a child wants to pray, he just does.

How does a child know how to pray? How does he form his concept of a God? I have been interested in religious life since childhood. As a young psychiatrist at Georgetown University Medical Center, I had the privilege to begin my exploration of these and other questions with the religious and the non-religious patients that were assigned to me. Some came for treatment of spiritually related issues, such as a crisis of religious identity, difficulty within an intermarried family, and even issues of demonic/spiritual possession. It became apparent during my training that these "religious" problems often had a psychological substrate. Conversely, the religious life of a patient (or lack there-of) often proved to be pivotal in the treatments of apparently unrelated psychiatric complaints, such as depression, anxiety disorders, and substance abuse. I decided then and there to incorporate questions about the patient's faith, beliefs, and religious life into my diagnostic interview. At that time, interest in religion within the psychiatric circles was minimal and there was a general tendency to disregard religious life altogether. In the last few years much has changed. Increasing numbers of psychiatrists, social workers, and other mental health professionals now recognize the validity of studying the spiritual lives of patients, both children and adults. Thinkers such as Robert Coles, *The Spiritual Life of Children* (1990) and Ana-Maria Rizzuto, *The Birth of the Living God* (1979) have helped legitimize this field of inquiry.

When I work (or rather, play) with my young patients, I ask them, Do they pray? When do they pray? And, What is God like for them? Often, the answers to the questions about religion provide me with valuable insights about their family dynamics and their relationship with the world. That is because the two — family dynamics and religious concepts — are often closely intertwined. The experiences children have with religion often reflect the experience they have with their parents.

The emergence of religious feelings in children and, subsequently, in the adults they become, has its roots in the infantile longings of a child for the ultimate protection and love of his big Other (most of the time, Mother). It is later elaborated by the magical thinking of the young child, who can easily imagine a world governed by an omnipotent being. Later, the dynamics of identification with the family and individuation from it, continue to shape the child's religious belief.

INFANTILE LONGINGS

Spiritual life begins as a yearning for the warmth and the safety of the all-providing Other, initially represented by the breast (or bottle). An infant, being totally helpless, is consumed by his physical discomforts — hunger, gas, cold, etc., and their relief. His sense of comfort and well-being comes from his needs being met. He begins to sense the maternal in the world through his mother.

While initially unable to separate between self and other, eventually the infant comes to recognize the presence of a separate other, which is the source of the comfort and satiation of his needs. This growing cognitive awareness of the differentiation of self and other, of me and her, adds urgency to his longing for this other. He feels small and needy in relation to the big and all-providing mother (or other caretaker), and he integrates into his psyche the knowledge that he can receive comfort, and have his needs met by, a powerful other. This initiates his longing for that powerful other.

The memory of this longing is carried out throughout the child's life and into adulthood. In the Catholic tradition, the worship of Mary resonates with this early longing, both for children and adults. Who else, but the mother of Jesus, the Ultimate Mother, would better serve to reassure and soothe that hunger for the closeness and safety which was provided by mother in infancy? A penitent praying to Mary is not alone anymore. He gives her the capacity to hold and love him like mother, thereby re-enacting the internalized drama of early life.

The Jewish tradition has its own feminine entity known as the

Shechinah. The Shechinah is the aspect of God which is most intimate with human beings. Jewish mystical practice (like other mystical practices) includes intense and ecstatic prayer which is
designed to bring forth a state of consciousness in which the initiated feels attachment to God. This attachment is not unsimilar in
nature to the attachment of the infant to his mother.

Children, however, do not require such involved practices in
order to find access to a caring and maternal God. They are very
close to their own feelings of smallness and the wish for protection, warmth, and love, and can achieve this feeling of closeness to
God fairly easily. I am reminded of a seven-year-old patient who
was involved in an accident which left her pinned under a car.
Alone and unable to move under the weight of the car, she prayed
to God and was able to find courage and solace in her belief that
she was not alone, and that God would save her.

MAGICAL THINKING

The developmental phenomenon of magical thinking is another influential factor in the formation of religious beliefs. Magical
thinking is a normal developmental process, seen commonly in
the preschool child. It is characterized by poor boundaries, pro-
jections of fantasy life onto the world (and self) and dramatic role
playing that feels so real to the child, and yet can shift at a
moment's notice. An example of such thinking is the tendency of
some preschoolers to invent an imaginary friend, whom they con-
jure up when needed, and send away when no longer required.
(For an extensive discussion of magical thinking see *The Magic
Years* by Selma H. Fraiberg, 1956.)

Children utilizing magical thinking believe that others can read
their thoughts or that they can influence events in the world
through the power of their thoughts and wishes. The rules of cause
and effect are suspended in favor of fantasy. A typical magical

fantasy, for instance, is the belief of the little child that his Mommy just came into the room because he wanted her there.

Given this universal tendency, it is not difficult for preschool, and even school age children, to believe in a God who oversees, loves, and protects them. And for some children, who possess especially strong magical thinking, the notion of an omnipotent and prescient God presents no problem whatsoever.

Magical thinking can be a source of unhappiness in the spiritual economy of some children, particularly those suffering from obsessive compulsive disorder (OCD). A child with this disorder exaggerates normal magical thinking into a harsh caricature of itself. Gone is the playfulness and fun — the excitement and humor of the normative developmental moment. In obsessive compulsive disorder, the child magically "knows" that something terrible will soon happen if he fails to perform a specific act. This act becomes the compulsion, which can ward off the evil, if only for a short time.

Common fears which preoccupy the OCD child include the notion that robbers are poised to enter the house, that a sudden fire is bound to erupt in the home, or that the death of her parents is imminent. These fears take on a magical quality on two counts. First, that it is destined to happen to her family, and second, that she, alone, has the power to forestall the event.

Sometimes the obsessive compulsive behavior takes on religious overtones, leading to excessive praying and a need to atone for imaginary sins. One poignant case involves an eleven-year-old girl who suffered from OCD and carried the awful thought that her parents would die because of something she had done in the past. This youngster had not done anything terribly wrong, nor had she been abused or treated badly by her family; it was her illness, pure and simple, which caused these feelings. She prayed to God reflexively and often, asking for the removal of the "devil" within, and often confessed that she herself deserved punishment.

THE WISH FOR AUTHORITY AND ORDER

Children experience being small in the world not only by virtue of their physical smallness and their dependence on adults for survival, but also because of their reliance on adults to provide structure and meaning. They worry about the dictates of the grownups in their lives — Mother, Father, Teacher, and so on, just as adults may worry whether God is running the world fairly. And they look to the grownups to set the rules that create the stability and meaning which they need. The cognitive leap from Mother, Father, and Teacher to God requires little effort for young people, particularly if they grow up in a somewhat religious home.

THE FAMILY MYTH

All families are small systems of meaning. Each family has its rules, its customs and its myths. The verbal as well as the non-verbal messages that a child receives at home, help construct her world view. The subtleties of religious belief are part of this family matrix.

The way a child experiences the relationship between her parents and herself, and her perception of safety and consistency (or lack thereof) in the home, contribute greatly to her perception of the world and of God.

For children growing up in chaotic and abusive homes, where they often don't know what to expect from their parents, God might well be "mad" to paraphrase Geertz. How many children of substance-abusing parents come home not knowing whether or not a parent will be in a rage or dramatically withdrawn? This uncertainty has a significant impact on children, which can spill over into their religious life. In families that seem outwardly religious and wholesome, but are in reality abusive and chaotic, the dissonance between reality and appearance may be too much for the children to assimilate, and they end up distancing themselves from religion altogether. Over the years I have seen many such people, who, having distanced themselves from their families, reject their parent's faith, as if God was as unreliable as their impaired parents.

Alternatively, people who come from abusive homes and turn to organizations such as Alcoholics Anonymous, are presented with a belief in a reliable and trustworthy God who provides structure, forgiveness, and guidance. This belief seems to help many people overcome their harsh history and find in God what they couldn't find in their parents.

A healthy, robust structure in a family goes a long way toward the psychological health of children. There is no substitute for being loved by parents who are fair and involved. The world by extension (magical thinking) also feels manageable then, and God is perceived as loving and approachable. A young patient of mine, who had been brought up in a completely secular home but was surrounded by the love and devotion of her parents, developed her own theology when she was confronted with the loss of both of her grandmothers. Her theology included the notion of an afterlife and a belief in overseeing and loving angels, spirits, and the movement of souls from earth to heaven. Even though her parents were not religious, this girl integrated the positive feelings of her upbringing into religious feelings that helped comfort her in her loss. She used prayer to continue to communicate with her grandmothers.

For most people, religious life begins with an identification with their parents. If they have been brought up in a reasonably loving family, they integrate the values and inclinations found at home. Baptists become Baptists, Jews become Jews, and Muslims become Muslims. This process is as much sociological as psychological. The child looks up to her parents and sees who they are praying to. A forgiving Jesus or a punitive God? Over time she metabolizes these values as her own.

Autonomous Strivings

Developmental psychology is really the story of the push/pull of two great forces struggling within the growing child. The first is the wish for closeness and the second is the urgent drive for autonomy. A non-specialist can see this every day with children. Consider the pleasure of the toddler as he runs *away* from his mother only to be followed by the equal and opposite pleasure of running back into her waiting arms — a game that, to forgive the pun, has legs.

As much as the child wishes to identify with a parent, he also feels the need to differentiate himself from her. The underlying dynamic is very interesting. The greater the need for closeness, the more intensely the child feels pressured to differentiate and be somehow different in the world. This plays out in both modest and dramatic ways when it comes to faith. In the case of the girl mentioned above, autonomous strivings led this girl to find her own theology, which felt correct, even if it was not taught at home.

There are children who become religious despite having received no religious training by their parents and there are children who become irreligious despite growing up in religious families. A child will sometimes use religious belief, or lack thereof, as a way to individuate and differentiate herself from the family. Rejecting or embracing a God is a relatively safe method for a child to establish a unique identity, separate from that of her parents.

A child may also wish to separate from his family's belief system if that home has been particularly unhappy. An extreme and dramatic example of such an alternative religious commitment can be found in the case of David, a fourteen-year-old boy whom I treated a number of years ago. David grew up in a "religious" home. His father was the priest of a Christian cult. His method of instilling Christian values in David involved arbitrary violence and abuse. The image of Jesus and good Christian teachings were mixed in David's mind with terrible and regular beatings. As a consequence David rejected his father's religion and became a Satanist. David believed that God was a seductive trickster who wooed people into needing Him, only to punish them with pain and illness, and then require them to make amends in order to be reprieved. Satan, in David's mind, was the good guy who exposed God for the "sadist" that He really was. Substitute David's father for God and David for Satan and the psychology of this theology becomes clear. Unfortunately, David also identified with the sadistic role of his father yielding terrible unhappiness, both for himself and others around him.

In conclusion, although prayer has nascent origins in the infantile, it has the potential to become a force that can transform a person's life and foster maturity. As James Hollis points out in *The Eden Project* (1998), the love between a man and a woman may emerge from similar infantile roots, as lovers seek the "magical other." But no one would suggest that marriage is infantile. So too, prayer, which begins with infantile feelings, and magical thinking, can grow to become a profound way of perceiving meaning, and even a force that inspires us to transform the world into a better place.

Prayer and Life

SAMUEL H. MILLER

When we are born into this world, it is not long before we are introduced to the pleasure and problem of communicating with people. There is something in the human individual that wants to express itself and to receive an answer from another person. Very early in our infancy we begin to utilize all manner of things such as symbols, gestures, and actions to communicate to others some of our impulses and wants.

After a time, we begin to use language, however falteringly or clumsily, to express ourselves. Through the use of language our wants and impulses and hopes and aspirations are clarified and communicated, answered and responded to, and thereby enriched by the people who live around us. It is true that we have to find out how to use the words we inherit and, to some degree, we make them over to fit ourselves. All the while, underneath our language, there is something inside ourselves that wants to express itself and receive some answer from the outside and be enhanced and possibly glorified in an experience that cannot be known as an isolated individual. The character of our own experience, what we have known and suffered, what we have seen and heard, what we have thought and divined, all this, or the lack of it, enters into our words and language. So it is true that the character of the soul may be known by the conversation it keeps.

Moreover, as we learn to talk with one another, we grow to understand that there is something more to language than the mere speaking of it. The most talkative people are not always the wisest, and they are not always the the best communicators. One of the difficulties that we face today is that as we have relied more on mere words we have lost sight of our wisdom. We are a newspaper-ridden, magazine-monopolized generation; verbose, as William James put it, with verbalities.

Now if this is true of us on the human level, there is also something in us that wants to express itself, but that wants an answer not from another person but from God. We are born not only by the will of the flesh, which puts us in our place in the human race, and not only according to the will of the world, which puts us in our place in the social environment and in human intercourse, but we are also born with the stamp of eternity upon us. We call that eternity the soul, and the soul wants to express itself and to get an answer from its natural Companion and Creator, God Himself.

In modern times, we experience a severe disconnection from each other and from nature. Our communications are broken. This is one of the reasons why most of us live or work in cities, where we can be very close together, in the hope that by being close together we can reconnect in a vital relationship. Instead, cities, science, and educational sophistication have helped to broaden the gap. Moreover, we are separated from one another by the individualism of our culture. Often, when we come together in a group where we might share experiences we have in common, we find ourselves so thoroughly defended by cautions and reserves that we cannot do more than meet at the outer edges, rather than at the vital center. The rapid and abrupt social changes that have marked the arrival of the technological and nuclear age have separated us from the past, and we are no longer part of a tradition.

Preceding our current state of disconnection is the fact that Western Civilization has historically been separated from God. In short, we live in a disconnected culture and this makes prayer extremely difficult. We do not know how to bridge the gap between our finite selves and the Infinite and have lost the skill and wisdom to handle things by wholes rather than by their parts.

Yet we are born into the flesh and into a world where we are inescapably caught in infinite ramifications so complex that many observers say we are primarily a product of our environment and our genetic inheritance. They believe the iron hand of physical law holds us inevitably in its grip. There is truth to this. So much truth, in fact, that each one of us, by each act and deed, even by each thought and impulse, registers our will upon the whole life of the entire universe. The smallest thing we do has ramifications that ultimately affect the fate of all things. Just as dropping the smallest pebble in the sea does, in some infinitesimal way, affect the tides and waves on distant continents, so what you and I do in the secrecy of our hearts affects the whole of life.

Prayer is the acceptance of the interconnected condition of our life. Through prayer, we can accept this infinite series of ramifications and try to develop the kind of sensitivity and imagination that will consecrate our relationship to the ultimate end of life and the purpose that is in all things. Prayer is about remaining connected with the larger environment beyond our personal circle. Prayer is about admitting and confessing that we are inevitably tied to God because we are part of the world that God made. Even if we revolt against the world, think that it has no meaning, believe it makes no sense, and say, "I will have nothing to do with it," we are still related to the whole of the world and to the end of everything by our virtue of warfare against it.

Prayer is the assumption that we are related to God and to the ultimate end of His purposes and creation. Prayer takes up this vast burden, lifting it with imaginative insight, and creates a place for the self in the picture of life. Prayer transforms the relationship between the individual and God, and helps us to become a force for good in the world. Once the transformation is complete, we will speak the language of the eternal and the Infinite and will get an answer.

I suspect that the reason so many people find it frustrating to pray is that not only do we use the language of earth, which we have inherited and which we cannot avoid, but we have never employed it in the service of heaven. That is, our prayers have been earthly prayers for earthly ends without being consecrated to the higher purpose of the transformation and surrender of the self to the eternal and Infinite, the very purpose of Almighty God. Prayer is the whole self expressing itself to the whole of life in conversation. Just as in our human intercourse talkativeness does not mean communication, so in prayer the more words we use and the more often we pray have no connection with the vitality and validity of our prayers. Sometimes the best prayer has no words. Certainly prayer is not a sudden flinging of oneself into the presence of God with a veritable storm of words and then, without waiting for an answer, an equally abrupt rushing out of His presence, even before the words have ceased to sound.

No, the words of a prayer depend for their meaning on the

silences of the prayer, and if there are no silences we can well be sure that the words have no meaning. What is a conversation but a peculiar balance between keeping quiet and speaking?

Strangely, our talkative prayers lead us to assume that we must try to find God. Spiritually speaking, one discovers sooner or later that God is usually much more capable of finding us than we are of finding God. Prayer itself is the answer to God's searching for us. When we lift up our voices, it is because God is already at work in our lives.

Indeed, this is what the church means when it talks about the "prevenience" of God; namely, that God is always in an experience before we come to it, and, when we come to it, He, being already there, is willing to bless us. Bernard of Clairvaux (1090–1153) says in *On the Love of God*:

> Do you awake? Well, God is also awake. If you rise in the night time, if you anticipate to your utmost your earliest awaking, you will find Him waking — you will never anticipate His own awakeness. In such an intercourse you will always be rash if you attribute any priority and predominant share to yourself; for He loves both more than you, and before you love at all.

When we offer a prayer we offer it with God's grace, we offer it with God's strength, and we offer it because we have already been found by God.

Why is this true? We are held in the hands of these infinite ramifications and we cannot do anything that does not affect the ultimate end of all things and the whole of things. And if this is true, then it is also true that He who is the Lord of all this, who is in it and made it and seeks to develop it, shall not leave one single element in it without His care and concern. A colleague of mine used to say that in all creation the most responsive being must be

God. This idea describes God in human terms and by human values: the better the man, the more responsive He is. But God is so far greater in His responsiveness than anyone we have ever known that the comparison falls apart by its own weight.

"Prayer," someone once said, "is the work of free men, while work is the prayer of slaves." With a devotion to getting things done, we have made a world of great cities, high buildings, large bridges, and amazing systems of transportation and finances. Yet what will these accomplishments do for us if we lose touch with our spirit and its wisdom? Even a lost spirit can yearn for grandeur though it may express itself in a negative way. When such a spirit is corrupted in a materialistic society it yearns to possess limitless wealth.

Yet our spirit, which hungers after the Infinite and eternal and wants to hold a conversation with God, still trembles and yearns and agonizes in all things we do and seeks to have some satisfaction in communion. This communion is prayer, whether it be wordless, as in meditation; in broken language; or in action done with full intent and spiritual imaginativeness.

Prayer is a thousand things, but it is always the meeting of God and man, and at that moment, there is a peace that surpasses all our understanding and a joy that the world can never take away. Lay up for yourselves treasures in the Spirit where moth and rust doth not corrupt and where thieves cannot break through nor steal, for where your treasure is, there your heart will find peace and joy and the fulfillment of all the anguish of your soul.

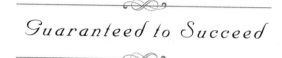

Guaranteed to Succeed

CHARLES SPURGEON

To seek aid in time of distress from a supernatural being is an instinct of human nature. I do not mean that human nature unrenewed ever offers truly spiritual prayer or exercises saving faith in the living God. But, like a child crying in the dark, with a painful longing for help from somewhere or other, the soul in deep sorrow almost always cries to some supernatural being for help. None have been more ready to pray in time of trouble than those who have ridiculed prayer in their prosperity. In fact, probably no prayers have been truer to the feelings of the hour than those that atheists have offered when in fear of death.

In one of his papers in *The Tattler*, Joseph Addison describes a man who, while a passenger on board a sailing ship, loudly boasted of his atheism. When a brisk gale sprang up, he fell on his knees and confessed to the chaplain that he had been an atheist. The common seamen, who had never heard the word "atheist" before, thought it was some strange fish. They were even more surprised when they learned out of his own mouth that the man never believed until that day that there was a God. One of the old sailors whispered to an officer that it would be a good deed to heave the man overboard, but this was a cruel suggestion, for the poor creature was already in misery enough. His atheism had evaporated, and in mortal terror he cried to God to have mercy on him.

Similar incidents have occurred more than once or twice. Indeed, so frequently does boastful skepticism tumble down at the end that we always expect it to do so. Take away unnatural restraint from the mind, and it may be said of all men that, like the comrades of Jonah, they cry "every man unto his God" (Jonah 1:5) in their trouble. As birds to their nests and as deer to their hiding places, so men in agony fly to a superior being for help in their hour of need.

By instinct man turned to his God in Paradise. Now, though man is to a sad degree a dethroned monarch, there lingers in his memory shadows of what he was and remembrances of where his strength must still be found. Therefore, no matter where you find a man, you will meet one who will ask for supernatural help in his distress.

I believe in the truthfulness of this instinct, and I believe that man prays because there is something in prayer. When the Creator gives His creature the power of thirst, it is because water exists to meet its thirst. When He creates hunger, there is food to correspond to the appetite. Even so, when He inclines men to pray, it is because prayer has a corresponding blessing connected with it.

We find a powerful reason for expecting prayer to be effective in the fact that it is an institution of God. In God's Word we are over and over again commanded to pray. God's institutions are not folly. Can I believe that the infinitely wise God has ordained for me an exercise that is ineffective and is no more than child's play? Does He tell me to pray, and yet does prayer have no more of a result than if I whistled to the wind or sang to a grove of trees? If there is no answer to prayer, prayer is a monstrous absurdity, and God is the author of it, which is blasphemy to assert. Only a fool will continue to pray once you have proved to him that prayer has no effect with God and never receives an answer. If it is indeed true that its effects end with the man who prays, prayer is a work for idiots and madmen and not for sane people!

I will not enter into any arguments upon the matter. Rather, I am coming to my text, which to me at least and to you who are followers of Christ, is the end of all controversy. Our Savior knew quite well that many difficulties would arise in connection with prayer that might tend to stagger His disciples, and therefore He has balanced every opposition with an overwhelming assurance. Read those words, "I say unto you." "I" — your Teacher, your Master, your Lord, your Savior, your God — "I say unto you, Ask, and it shall be given you; seek, and ye shall find; knock, and it shall be opened unto you" (Matthew 7:7 KJV).

In the text our Lord meets all difficulties first by giving us the weight of His own authority: "I say unto you." Next, He presents us with a promise: "Ask, and it shall be given you." And so on. Then He reminds us of an indisputable fact: "Every one that asketh receiveth." Here are three mortal wounds for a Christian's doubts about prayer.

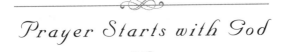

Prayer Starts with God

LLOYD JOHN OGILVIE

I want to share a revolutionary thought. It has changed my life. My whole perception of prayer has been transformed by it. As a result, my prayers and praying have become more exciting than ever.

I've been a Christian for forty-four years. For far too many of those years, I held a totally incorrect conception of prayer. I labored with the misapprehension that prayer was my idea, that my conversations with God were initiated by me. This idea burdened me with the belief that I had to get God's attention and that He would neither listen nor respond until I said the right words and led a life worthy of His attention. Prayer became laborious. Often, I was reluctant to pray when I needed it the most because of things I'd done or said that made me feel ashamed or embarrassed by my less than perfect life. My belief that prayer was initiated by me caused me to let my moods and spiritual readiness dictate when I would pray.

Then a few years ago, I happened on a combination of Scriptures from the Old and New Testaments that expanded my tight, constricted, and limited view of prayer. These words testified to a truth that I desperately needed to learn and to live.

Simply stated, the truth is this: prayer starts with God. It is His idea. Our desire to pray is the result of God's greater desire to talk with us. He has something to say when we feel the urge to pray. He is the initiator. Our keen desire to begin and end the day with prolonged prayer is His gift. When we feel a need to pray for challenges or opportunities throughout the day, it is because He has wisdom and insight He wants to impart. When we face crises and suddenly feel the urge to pray for strength, that feeling is a response to the Lord's invasion of our minds, which triggers the thought of needing help that is then congealed into our desire to pray. He, not us, is the author of our longing for His help.

The Scriptures that have caused this renaissance in my prayers tell us something magnificent about God and the wondrous way He has created us for communion and conversation with Him. He is the instigator, implementor, and inspiration of prayer.

THE ANSWER IS PREPARED BEFORE WE PRAY

In Isaiah 65:24, listen to what the Lord Himself tells us about prayer: "It shall come to pass that before they call, I will answer; and while they are still speaking, I will hear." This tells us that the answer to our prayers is prepared by the Lord before we pray. The desire to talk to the Lord about our needs comes from Him. Prayer begins in the mind of God, invades our minds, is formulated into a clarification of what He wants to do or give, and then is articulated in our words. He is more ready to hear than we are to pray!

This propitious promise from the Lord is made in response to an excruciating question asked by Israel, recorded in Isaiah 64:12. The people had sinned and felt the judgment of God. They felt distant from Him, though He had never left His people. Their sorrow reached its height when they cried out, "Wilt thou keep silent . . . ?" (RSV). The response of grace was mediated through the prophet Isaiah, who explains that there will come a time when not only will the Lord answer, but His answer will precede the petition, and prayer will be our response to God's call rather than just His response to our call. This prophetic revelation of the nature of prayer is in anticipation of the messianic age when God Himself would come to reconcile and redeem His people. The people to whom Isaiah wrote never fully appreciated the wondrous offer God made in this statement. It was only after the incarnation and Pentecost that a new creation was prepared to appropriate it. It was not until the liberation of the bondage of the will took place on Calvary and the new creatures in Christ were filled with His Spirit at Pentecost that a new Israel, the church, was born and could accept and utilize the awesome promise the Lord had made so long before.

Thomas Carlyle once said, "Prayer is and remains a native and deep impulse of the soul of man." That sounds lovely, but I don't believe it. No one naturally desires to pray. Our ability to choose to pray is debilitated until we are loved, liberated, and regenerated by Christ. It is after we have been transformed by the cross and filled with the Spirit that we can experience the enlivening of the "native and deep impulse" to pray. And even after we've been born again, it is the Lord who motivates us to pray. It is part of His prevenient (beforehand) grace. Not even the longing for God is our accomplishment. It is birthed in our souls by the Lord who created us for communion with Him.

Commenting on this promise in Isaiah, Luther said, "Our prayer pleases God because He has commanded it, made promises, and given form to our prayer. For that reason, He is pleased with our prayer, He requires it and delights in it, because He promises, commands, and shapes it. . . . Then He says, 'I will hear.' It is not only guaranteed, but it is actually already obtained."

HE IS THE IMPLEMENTOR OF PRAYER

At the same time I was pondering the implications of the Lord's offer in Isaiah, He led me to rediscover another passage that deepened my understanding of that promise. In 1 John 5:12–15, the Lord comes to us as the implementor of prayer. The apostle John asserts the secret of dynamic prayer in the context of our life in Christ when he says, "He who has the Son has life; he who does not have the Son of God does not have life" (verse 12). The apostle wanted his readers in the early church to be sure of their relationship, now and forever, in Christ. He stated that the reason he wrote was "that you may know that you have eternal life, and that you may continue to believe in the name of the Son of God" (verse 13). For John, the Son is Immanuel (God with us) and continues with us to guide us. John's Christian life was not an anxious searching for the Lord but a moment by moment response to God's impinging, invading presence. Then in verses 14 and 15, John sounds the same joyous note we heard in the Isaiah promise. "Now this is the confidence that we have in Him, that if we ask anything according to His will, He hears us. And if we know that He hears us, whatever we ask, we know that we have the petitions we have asked of Him."

I quickly checked the original Greek text to review John's words, which I had studied so often before in the Bible. Now they came alive in new vitality and freshness. The words for "confidence" and "in Him" leaped off the page. Confidence is *perresia* in Greek. That means boldness. It is a compound word made up of *pan*, meaning all, and *ressie*, meaning "to tell" or "freedom to speak boldly." Prayer is the freedom to speak freely and boldly to the Lord, who has instigated our prayer. Then I discovered that the English translation of the next words, again, do not catch the exciting implication of the original Greek. The confidence we have in prayer is what "we have in Him" or *Pros auton*, which really means "toward Him" or "face-to-face" with Him. *Pros* is from *prosopton*, which means "face." Prayer, for John, is face-to-face communication with Christ, which is part of the eternal quality of life we have in Him and gives us boldness. In this face-to-face communication, first we listen to Him intently and then we can speak with intrepidness.

And who starts the face-to-face conversation? The Lord! John makes that clear in 4:19: "We love Him because He first loved us." God is the prime mover in salvation, the giver of faith, and the initiator of prayer. In prayer, He makes His will known to us so that we can ask for what He longs to give. He calls us into His presence because He has the answer to our needs and questions. "If we ask anything according to His will, He hears us." Our assurance that He hears us is that He is the one who asked for the conversation. He would not call us to prayer and then refuse to listen or to be attentive to our prayer. Confidence and boldness are ours: prayer is our response to His call. During our face-to-face communion, He shows us what to ask for so that He can help us.

So when we pray, it is with the confidence that we are asking for what He is prepared to give us. "And if we know that He hears us, whatever we ask, we know that we have the petitions that we have asked of Him." We know He will hear us before we ask because the content of our asking has been guided by Him.

The same assurance is stated by John earlier in his epistle: "And by this we know that we are of the truth, and shall assure our hearts before Him. For if our heart condemns us, God is greater than our heart, and knows all things. Beloved, if our heart does not condemn us, we have confidence toward God. And whatever we ask we receive from Him, because we keep His commandments and do those things that are pleasing in His sight. And this is His commandment: that we should believe on the name of His Son Jesus Christ and love one another, as He gave us commandment" (1 John 3:19–23). The basics of prayer are already given in the commandment. The Lord reminds us of this as He calls us into prayer and then, as the instigator of prayer, spells out the specific details of how to believe and love in particular situations.

Allow me to illustrate. Recently one of my friends was in trouble. He needed my help, and yet he was not sure I had time to help him. So I asked one of my sons to talk to my friend and offer my help. My son said to him, "My dad really wants to help and he's willing to do the following things." He enumerated the personal and practical assistance I wanted to give. The intervention of someone as close to me as my son convinced my friend of my real heart in the matter. When the man came to me with his request, he did not have to wonder about my readiness to help. He came with confidence because he knew what I was willing to do.

Or, consider the process of negotiation in the business world. A man in my congregation told me that settling a difficult business matter is so much easier when he knows what the other person is willing to do. If he can get someone to intercede for him to determine the other party's terms, he can make an offer that he knows will be accepted. On the other hand, when he wants someone to bid at a price he is willing to accept, he gets an emissary to go to the bidder to disclose his willingness to sell and the price he is open to accept. When the offer comes, he responds because it complies with his terms.

Some years ago, I needed a grant from a large foundation for a strategic program at my church. A trusted friend interceded for me. He talked to the head of the foundation and arranged an interview for me. The man liked my idea and suggested how I should draft the proposal to be sure it was met with enthusiasm and approval by the foundation's board of directors. I followed his suggestions and the proposal was accepted and the grant was made. All the guesswork was taken out of my application. The foundation was responsible for distribution of funds provided by an American benefactor. It had to distribute the funds; all I had to do was prepare something that met the foundation's requirements. I could not have known how to do that without the help of the head of the foundation, who helped me ask in a way I could be confident would be accepted.

These examples hardly begin to illustrate the central truth John is seeking to communicate. Christ is the heart of God within us. He guides us in what and how to ask. When we ask in keeping with what He has revealed to us, we ask with boldness and the knowledge that the answer is on the way. "We know that we have the petitions that we have asked of Him." In the original Greek, the word "know," *oidamen*, is used twice: If we know that He hears us, then we know that we will receive what He has guided us to request. A. T. Robertson says in his book, *Word Pictures in the New Testament* (1930–33), that the Greek implies "the confidence of possession by anticipation."

INSPIRATION COMES FROM HIM

The third passage of Scripture that confirmed for me that prayer starts with God is Romans 8:26–30. In this passage the Spirit of the Lord, the present Christ, is the initiator of the desire, content, and assurance of prayer. Note how Paul develops this theme. "Likewise the Spirit also helps in our weaknesses. For we do not know what we should pray for as we ought, but the Spirit Himself makes intercession for us with groanings which cannot be uttered. Now He who searches the hearts knows what the mind of the Spirit is, because He makes intercession for the saints according to the will of God. And we know that all things work together for good to those who love God, to those who are called according to His purpose. For whom He foreknew, He also predestined to be conformed to the image of His Son, that He might be the firstborn among many brethren. Moreover, whom He predestined, these He also called; whom He called, these He also justified; and whom He justified, these He also glorified."

The full meaning of this passage is revealed by starting at the end. We are called and appointed to belong to the Lord. That election and call is according to His predestined plan. We do not choose; we are chosen. That is where it all begins. The Lord singles us out to belong to Him. As His children, He wants us to accept His love lavishly given on the cross and offered in the presence of His Spirit. He wants to make us like Himself. That requires the quality of the face-to-face communion that is prayer. His desire is for all things in our lives to work together to accomplish the plan He has for each of us. That plan is His will for us. The Greek word *thelema* is used to mean "will" in this passage. It also means desire. The Lord has a desire for all of us, a purpose for us to accomplish. But He does not leave us, after we are "born again," with no training or help in accomplishing this purpose of being conformed into His own image. He invades our subconscious with preconscious longings and urgings that are manifested in the conscious desire to pray and seek His desires for us. The Father, the Son, and the Holy Spirit are one. The Spirit is the reigning, glorified Christ within us. This is what Paul made undeniably clear to the Galatians. "And because you are sons, God has sent forth the Spirit of His Son into your hearts, crying out, 'Abba, Father!' " (Galatians 4:6). The Spirit of the Son comes to us in our weaknesses. He calls us to prayer and then gives us the "groanings which cannot be uttered." What does this mean? My understanding is that the groanings are the preconscious longings and urgings, which He articulates through us by helping us find the words that reveal these longings in prayer. It is not that the intercession is done for us, for that would deny the purpose for our cooperation with the Lord. First, the invasion of His Spirit produces our longing to pray. Then, when we feel the need to pray but still don't know how or what to pray, He guides us in our prayers. Because He knows our hearts and He is the heart of the Lord, He brings our hearts in harmony with His own. His purpose is to bring our desires into alignment with His desires so we can be part of all things working together for good.

Recently I had a misunderstanding with a cherished friend that seemed to end our relationship. I was startled to realize that, for a time, I didn't want to reconcile with my friend. I chalked it up to irreconcilable differences that precluded the possibility of forgiveness and a new beginning. I was hurt and angry. My plan was to forget the whole mess. Some weeks later, an uneasiness began to grow in me. I couldn't shake the memory of my friend from my mind. That was followed by a mysterious desire to pray about him. When I responded to the inner urgings to pray, I noticed a difference in my attitude. As I prayed, I was given new empathy for what might have caused my friend's behavior. I was given a completely different picture of his needs; and then I asked for a way to communicate acceptance and forgiveness. As I lingered in prayer, a strategy for what I needed to do and say became clear. I had the deep conviction that the plan came from the Lord. Therefore, when I asked for His help to accomplish His will in the matter, I could ask with boldness. The inner disquiet, like an inaudible wordless groaning, turned into charity and was articulated in my request for the strength to do what the Lord had promised He would do through me, if I were willing. I felt a new "will" working in my imagination to form a picture of how a reconciliation would be accomplished. The Lord was initiator and inspiration from start to finish.

The same process occurred regarding a tough decision I had to make recently. I thought I knew what the Lord wanted and did not pray a lot about it. When the decision was made, I had no peace. There was a jangling static in my spirit. It lasted for days. When my sleep was interrupted by the disturbance, I knew something was very wrong. I asked the Lord to be very clear. I asked Him how to pray. A specific request was given me to make. I asked that, if the disturbance was from Him, it would continue and grow. However, if the decision I made was right and the disquiet was simply my own fear of implementing it, I was led to ask that the disturbance be taken away. The static proceeded to rise to an unbearably high decibel. That led me to confess, "Lord, now I know I'm on the wrong track. Show me what you want me to do." After hours of quiet listening, I reversed my hastily made decision. As I prayed, a new direction formed in my mind. When I decided to follow the new direction, the jangling static inside me subsided. An inner calm and confidence grew in its place. Then with holy boldness, I asked for what the Spirit had formed in my mind. When I asked, I knew that I was assured of the answer. Subsequently, the decision was worked out by the Spirit's power exactly as He detailed it in prayer. Again, He had been the source of the disturbance, the desire to review the previous decision, the architect of the new plan, the communicator of the different direction, and the instigator of a boldness to ask for what He had imparted.

Our desire to pray is the result of God's call to prayer. He has something to say. Our responsibility is to listen to what He wants to give us in response to our problems and potentials. He will make it clear. Then we can say with boldness:

I sought the Lord, and afterward I knew
     He moved my soul to seek Him, seeking me;
It was not I found, O Savior true,
     No, I was found of Thee.
                    [Author unknown]

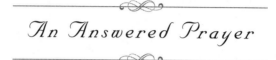

An Answered Prayer

ANTHONY STERN, M.D.

*P*rayer opens us. It deepens our faith, our love, and our humility. It exposes us to the truth of our lives — of our time bound, event filled lives — and to the Timeless Life underlying all, encompassing all, and connecting us all.

Prayer leaves its trace on our lives in two basic ways, through the mystery of spiritual opening and through tangible incidents when time and the Timeless seem to intertwine, or are revealed as one. The first kind of trace can be sensed as an uplifting, perhaps even a challenging, feeling, or is hardly sensed at all. The second trace unfolds on the surface, as it were, as an event that can be described more readily.

Here is an example. It was August of 1980. I was twenty-six years old, about to begin medical school, and working as a counselor at a skiing and tennis camp in Austria. I'd drifted into a state of inner distress in part because I had strong and mixed feelings about starting medical school. Although I'm usually more or less gregarious, that summer in particular I felt a real need for solitude.

A RETREAT AND A PRAYER

Early one evening after dinner I took two hours off and walked up a hillside near the camp. The shadows were lengthening. The coolness of dusk felt soothing. I sat on the forest floor surrounded by tall pine trees. I was silent for a time, breathing in the mountain air and the fragrance of the trees. I softly sang to myself former Beatle George Harrison's song "My Sweet Lord." And then I felt an urge to pray.

"Dear Father," I began in a quiet voice. "Please help me. I need to know that you're present. If you're there, let me know. If you can't come yourself, send a message. Please let me know you're there."

It was a heartfelt, spontaneous prayer.

I stood and walked around a little. By the time I made my way home, it was dark.

A RESPONSE OUT OF THE BLUE

The answer to my prayer arrived at an unexpected time and through an unlikely source. It also came in a rather American style that I would never have predicted — in a slang form that was so casual, so brief and lighthearted and to the point that it could well have been construed as flippant. Yet for me, this lighthearted style enhanced the message, because it expressed a good-natured and reassuringly playful feeling. Religious sages have often pointed to God's presence in an unexpected turn of events.

And who is to say the Divine doesn't also have a capacity for blunt simple talk as well as a finely honed wit — or, for that matter, a questionable sense of humor at times?

In any case, what happened was this: I was sitting in the sunshine with a few campers after lunch the next day; we were joking and making small talk. I was in a mellow, sociable, vaguely sleepy haze — quite a different state of mind from the prior evening's prayerful longing. One of the campers, a fifteen-year-old boy, suddenly turned to me in the midst of our thoroughly mundane chatter and reported, "Dad says Hi."

It was like a feather's touch. It hardly registered.

"Excuse me?" I asked absentmindedly. "What did you say?"

Again he said, "Dad says Hi."

It started to register as I warmed to this unusual detour in the conversation. "Who, your dad?"

"No."

"My dad?"

"No."

"Whose, then?"

"No one's in particular. Just Dad," he said emphatically, yet with a sense of bewilderment.

I smiled at this prophet before me. My own surprise and delight was still just beginning to reach consciousness. "What are you talking about?"

He shrugged and laughed. "I don't know."

REFLECTIONS

As I have considered my evening prayer and the conversation the next day, I realize that I have had three responses to the episode: skepticism, acceptance, and disregard. The skeptical part of me has trouble believing that it really happened — that anything like that could happen. But another larger part of me responds with simple acceptance. I prayed to my Heavenly Father, and in His loving-kindness, He answered me.

I'm reminded of the story about the eighteenth-century mystic Rabbi Levi Yitzhak of Berditchev, whose father-in-law objected when he turned toward the Hasidic teachings. The father-in-law tells him he will forgive this stupidity if only Levi Yitzhak will explain to him what he has learned from his Hasidic master that is so special. In reply Levi Yitzhak says he received the knowledge that there is a God in Heaven who created the world.

The father-in-law was a pious Jew. "Who doesn't know that?" he asks. "Everyone knows that." Rabbi Levi Yitzhak replies, "A lot of folks think it and even more of them say it. Only through my master have I really learned it."

I don't claim to have "really learned it" for good — my faith still wavers all the time — but the experience I had in 1980 was surely a step in the right direction.

At the same time, I have had another important response to this event, one that's been just as central: and that is to simply disregard it. It's perhaps the most common response we humans have to such events. As a Harvard undergraduate, I took a course on the Bible with Northrop Frye, a visiting professor well known in the field of literary criticism. At one point he made a noteworthy comment concerning the miracles of Jesus. The question is not did they occur, Frye suggested, but if we had been there, would we have seen them? Then there is a further question, the one most relevant here: If we had seen the miracles, what would have been their effect on us? Would we have allowed the essence of their message and their challenge to penetrate our being? Would we have lived with a keen awareness of the good news about the Spirit that they convey?

Reflecting on the "Dad says Hi" incident, I ask myself these questions: Have I let this event truly penetrate? My answer: I come up at least a bit short. Have I struggled to look into its meaning as fully as I could, and to live by it? Not as wholeheartedly as I might have. Have I even *doubted* the event with sufficient intensity? Not really. Happily, writing this essay provides me with another opportunity to examine my response.

In fact, until midway into writing this essay I hadn't recognized the degree of my disregard. It is often said that the greatest enemy of the spiritual life is not doubt or skepticism, but indifference. That is what I mean by the word "disregard." Jesus' words in Revelation come to mind: "I wish you were one or the other, but since you are neither hot nor cold, but only lukewarm, I will spit you out of my mouth" (3:15–16 NJB).

Illuminating events such as the one I experienced in Austria remind me to renew my faith, even as they also throw light on my shortcomings. One way or the other, prayer shows us that the universe is fundamentally a friendly and caring place. Religious faith of almost any denomination tells us that this benevolence lives at the tender core of our being.

Undeniably, the universe can also be tragic, cruel, and seemingly indifferent. That fact can often be confusing, in addition to the sheer pain it causes in us. And the question "Why do we suffer?" takes on a new level of perplexity when we have had a glimpse of the complete Goodness at the heart of things.

I can sympathize with the reader who feels skeptical about life, because the skeptical part of me, though a little sobered, remains mostly unconvinced. And up to a point I honor that doubt in me and in others, because it resonates with one undeniable characteristic of the universe — the characteristic of randomness.

What does it actually mean, however, to honor this doubt? To accept it in a passive way doesn't do it justice. Some great religious teachers propose that honoring one's doubt involves wrestling actively with it, in fact with the whole of one's being, and in so doing to feel one's way into the massive uneasiness at the heart of the doubt.

CAN GOD TALK TO US?

This is what I think: God gives us answers if we ask seriously — if we keep on seeking, really keep on knocking. The truth of the matter may be even stranger still: that God offers continual answers regardless of what we do, though we may not understand them; that the whole unfolding of our lives is nothing but a two-way conversation with the Source of all, though most of us resist this reality; and that there is nothing, in other words, but grace.

It is tempting to try to distinguish between "real" moments of communication with the Divine, as illustrated by the spiritual quests of the saints and masters, and the shaky or "false" ones that occur in the lives of more "average" folks like you or me or our cousins or neighbors. But I think any experience of the Divine Mystery is essentially valid. At the same time, any spiritual experience is also incomplete and imperfect. Since we are all human, our views of such communications are more or less lacking and more or less muddled. We easily misinterpret. We all too quickly jump to conclusions and then remain stuck in them. Our fear and pride create shells around us, which in turn distort and limit the fullness of life.

Most of us, often without even knowing it, hold all too tenaciously to the ideas and feelings that arise from our first encounters in life, whether spiritual or otherwise. Prayer slowly loosens that hold. Prayer opens us to the Source of our lives, and this Source continues to surprise us with ever more delicate promptings and ever more profound teachings. Less and less obstructed by our own tensions and opinions, we start to see more steadily into the core of our experiences, the core of our truths, and the core of the Mystery. And this, all of this, is the life of prayer.

Fleeing or Following Jesus to the Cross

LEO J. O'DONOVAN, S.J.

Note: In considering the unifying theme of this book, the power of prayer, I reflected on the many ways the gospels inspire us to participate in a kind of prayer to and with the Lord. Each of us prays because we believe in the mystery of salvation, because we seek a connection with the God who gave God's own life for us. Relating the story of the passion of Christ, the Gospel of Mark invites us to accompany Jesus to the cross and reimagine the death that has brought each of us the promise of new life, a promise that is the foundation of all our prayer.

*A*mong the Gospel narratives of the passion and death of Jesus of Nazareth, none is darker or more dramatic than the Gospel of Mark (14:1-15:47). In many Christian churches throughout the world, it is read each Lent on the Sunday before Easter, often known as Passion or Palm Sunday. But it is also there for us to read and ponder at all times.

This sacred text bears a story to us through time, and beyond time, in which the last days of Jesus of Nazareth are recounted. It embodies the mystery of salvation for all who call Jesus Lord and thus bears with it the grace of God's own saving love and life. As such, it is, quite literally, inexhaustible. God's own spirit turns us to read and hear it again and again, to learn from it, to be challenged by it, consoled as well as warned, made aware anew of how destructive we human beings can be while also recognizing, in Jesus, God's answer to such evil.

No proclamation or reading of this text will ever give its full meaning, just as heaven alone will bring us face to face with the fullness of God's love in Christ. And yet it happens that each time we hear or read the Gospel narrative of the passion, we may gain new insight into its saving mystery through reflection on one or another moment in the story. Let me, accordingly, draw your attention to the ending of the scene in which Jesus is arrested in the Garden of Gethsemane. Betrayed by Judas, He is accosted by a Roman guard and led away to trial. And then we read the dreadful words concerning the disciples who had come with Him to pray; after having spent so much time in His radiant company, "with that, all deserted him and fled" (Mark 14:50).

On hearing or reading these words, still more on reimagining the scene in its awful concrete detail, grief, sorrow, and deep mourning seem befitting responses. Silence and mournful contemplation seem in order, not further helpless words.

But the Spirit of God gathers the church on every Palm Sunday to recall and to relive the passion of Jesus. And we must, however stumblingly, speak of it. Palm Sunday is the great day of paradox in the Christian church, as it has been for centuries. Throughout the world on this day, the liturgy begins with a moment of exaltation. The Master is greeted at the gates of Jerusalem as the one in whom God's true reign will dawn. A colt to carry a King is procured for Him; disciples clothe the colt and lay branches before it to signal the King's triumphant entrance into the city.

The day begins, thus, with exaltation and continues through the reading of the passion and the congregation's participation in it through communion. Later in the week, in the sacred triduum, the humiliation of Jesus is re-enacted in the church. We listen again, obediently, to the message of our salvation — in the hope that the exaltation of the resurrection will be real for us because we have accompanied Jesus to Jerusalem and to His cross. For surely, unless we go with Him his way of the cross, we cannot go with Him through resurrection to God in eternity.

Each time we read the passion of Christ, but especially on Palm Sunday and in Holy Week, we are urged to let Jesus go to the cross for us. He did this for each of us and all of us, for our parents and ourselves, for our children and their teachers, for our daily concerns, and our friends who are sick. And so He is our friend.

But He did this also for every human being, for friends and foes alike, for the leaders of nations, and especially, for the poor, for us all as human beings. "For those at peace and those at war, for young and old, and every race." And so He is the Lord.

And He did this, above all, for the God whom He called Father — whom today, because we seek a language and a culture that embraces equality, we might call the Parent of us all. He did it for the one He called Father. He went to the cross for God.

In the company of His disciples, before the threat of authorities secular and religious, He went to the cross for you and for me and for each of us individually. All the sorrow, all the betrayal and the desertions, and the sickness of our human condition, He took upon Himself for us. The suffering, the subjection to powers beyond our control. All the burden of being human. The frustrations, the failures, the folly, the foolishness, the waste, the anxiety of my life, the agony of yours. The resentments, the recriminations, the jealousies, the fruitless sacrifices and the foolish selfishness, and yes, finally, death itself. All this, the Man of Sorrows took upon Himself for us. For you, for each and every one of us. For me.

There is a great tradition in late medieval German art that shows Jesus surrounded by the instruments of the passion before His crucifixion. Here He sits disconsolate, crowned by thorns, battered by reeds, adorned by the purple cloak. It was not entirely accurate, of course, to set this Man of Sorrows apart from the story as whole. And yet the image is unforgettable, precisely because His sorrow was so great — because He did take every sorrow you and I have ever experienced or could know upon Himself. For each of us.

He also took upon Himself for all of us, for the whole human family, the conflicts and oppression, the hopes of peace dashed by terrorism, the bloody wars, the massacres, the genocide, the persecution and discrimination, the malevolent festering of one people's pride against another. He took upon Himself hunger and famine, abuse of power, neglect of the poor, indifference to children, coldness to strangers, recurrent, horrific hostility to others who are different. All this, the Man of Sorrows took upon Himself for us all. For the human community.

We will never appreciate the depths of His dedication without reimagining His story again and again in our mind's eye, guided by the church's prayer and symbolism and teaching. And then, little by little, the conviction grows.

He knew all of this. He knew my sorrow and sin. He knew your sorrow and suffering and sin. Not in its particularity, nor in every detail. Jesus knew and understood the world emblematically through fundamental experience and living, through the utter dedication of His innocent life lived before His Father for His fellow human beings. Through an innocence lived for others and for God, His life could overcome, because it was so pure, all the waywardness from which He turned. Through facing disappointment and despair, oppression and lovelessness, betrayal and distrust, yes, all our darkness and all our sin, He could know, as Scripture tells us, "what was in the human heart" (John 2:25).

He knew what was in the human heart, and He opened that heart once and for all to God. As we never could. For you, for me, for all of us, for God.

We cannot save ourselves, however generous we seek to be. And on Palm Sunday, at the beginning of Holy Week, and each time we read the story of the passion of Jesus, we must above all learn to let Jesus save us. In our hope to know the joy of His resurrection.

But before we imagine or begin to hope for that joy, we must let Him go to the cross for us. Let us watch and follow and wait and mourn and know His sorrows. And as we watch, let us stand humbled by remembering the awful words: "With that, all deserted Him and fled."

CHAPTER FOUR

A Path to Understanding

I have been driven many times to my knees by the overwhelming conviction that I had nowhere else to go. My own wisdom, and that of all about me, seemed insufficient for the day.

— ABRAHAM LINCOLN

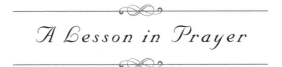

A Lesson in Prayer

SUE BENDER

Dear reader: So much of how I write has to do with the way words look on the page. My essay is set a little differently in order to convey a sense of order and calm. I hope you enjoy it. — Sue Bender

Following "a path that has heart" — taking it wherever it led — brought me to the Amish. A tremendous need led my spirit, guiding me in ways I often didn't understand. I set out on an unfamiliar path toward an unknown conclusion, filled with fear and doubt. I was hoping for answers but kept coming back to the question, What really matters?

Recently, when New World Library first invited me to write about prayer, I thought, "Why me? I'm not an expert."

Now, after much thinking, I'm still not an expert.

What I am learning doesn't fit my original stereotype of prayer. But the invitation gave me a chance to examine this journey of the spirit to try to find words describing what I might know about prayer. I immediately looked up prayer in the dictionary:

"an approach to deity in word or thought
the act or practice of praying to God."

When I first went to live with the Amish many years ago, if anyone had suggested I was trying to make sense of my life, I would have vehemently said, "No." I would have said, "I'm lucky. I have nothing to be dissatisfied about. I have a husband whom I love and who loves me, two fine sons, friends, and work I enjoy." If I had been aware, I would have understood that I didn't think I had any right to be unhappy.

Living with the Amish introduced me to prayer.

The first thing we did very early each morning was pray for five minutes. We knelt in the living room. "Thank you, God, for all your help. Forgive us our sins, help us with the land." In my honor they said the prayer in English, rather than their German dialect. Each day ended the same way.

Five minutes of prayer.

They modeled a way to pray, a way of being with prayer that was different from anything I had ever seen, felt, or experienced. Their daily prayer ritual, in itself, wasn't unusual. What was unusual was that they spent the rest of their day living what they believed. There was no separation between prayer and action.

They modeled a way to put prayer into action.

The very first day, as I entered the house that was to be my home for seven weeks, I noticed a difference. The rooms themselves weren't unusual. I walked into a large sunny kitchen, with its central table, black-metal wood-burning stove, linoleum floor, and speckled beige Formica counters — nothing distinctive, neither old-fashioned nor modern.

But the room glowed.

The feeling went beyond everyday cleanliness and order. The air felt alive, almost vibrating. Can a room have a heartbeat? Can a space be serene and exciting at the same time? I'd never felt a room like that. Their care and intention created a space that felt sacred.

I usually walk around in an excited state, my mind racing, but after a few minutes in that Amish kitchen, I slowed down and felt calm surround me. The difference was so dramatic that I wondered if I had entered an altered state of consciousness.

After living with my Amish family for three days I felt I *had* entered an *Alice in Wonderland* reality.

It was surprisingly easy to adjust to the fact that they drove a horse and buggy instead of a car; had no TV, radio, microwave, or other modern conveniences; or dressed in 19th-century clothing. What was startling was:

No one rushed.

Whatever they were doing, whatever the task, each step was done with care. They moved through the day unhurried. They didn't rush to finish so they could move on to the "important things." For them all work was important, in and of itself.

That's when I began learning their *way* of prayer. Doing the dishes, mowing the lawn, baking bread, quilting, canning, hanging out the laundry, picking fresh produce — all were a chance to be close to God.

No distinction was made between the sacred and the everyday. It was all ordinary. It was all sacred.

The Amish practiced daily what they believed. They never preached to me. They never said, "Our way is better." Deed, not words, mattered. How they lived day in, day out reflected their faith. They modeled a *way* to be — a way I admired — something to aim for.

"Why is Amish land so beautiful?" I asked one evening. "What makes it feel special? I'm a city person, Eli, and I didn't see a cow until I was twelve. I don't know where the sun sets, or how to tell which way the wind blows, or distinguish one crop from another, but I have eyes, and I trust my heart. This land is loved."

"The land is God's," Eli said. "It's my job, and the job of every Amish person, to take care of it for Him. Caring for the land, every day, is my way to be close to God. His land must be honored." As he talked, I could feel his relationship with God and the land, expressed in an infinite number of ways. They lived their prayer. Their whole life was their practice.

As I remembered my conversation with Eli, I thought of one of the definitions I had just read for prayer:

"an approach to deity in word or thought."

After living with the Amish I would add: an approach to deity in word or thought or *deed*.

◦◦◦

Who is richer? I wondered.

My life was so rich and varied in some ways but poor and disconnected in others. Their neighbors had a security I didn't. In times of sickness, accident, financial setback, or natural disaster, they knew support would be there.

Brotherly love is their insurance.

◦◦◦

Following a "path of the heart" offers many lessons.

My definition of prayer has grown larger — vast. I am also learning there are so many more ways to pray than I had ever imagined.

A friend once told me about the "home" he and his family had as refugees in Europe during World War II. He, his mother, and younger brother moved constantly from place to place, from a hotel, to an inn, to a friend's home, and back to a hotel again. Each time they arrived in a new place, his mother would open the small suitcase that held all their belongings and bring out the lace tablecloth she had used for their Friday night meals in Poland, before they were forced to leave and begin their flight.

In each place the ritual was exactly the same. She would place the suitcase on a table, carefully drape the tablecloth over the suitcase, light a candle, and in that moment, their room, wherever it was, became *home*.

This ritual was their prayer.

My day begins at 4:30 or 5:00 A.M. Before reading the newspaper, I read one page in each of five small "inspirational" books. The books change, but they are always ones that remind me I am not alone, that a spirit larger than myself is at work, a universe larger than my immediate self-interest and concerns. For that I am endlessly grateful.

In thinking about prayer, I remembered a conversation I once had with the women in the first Amish community I lived in. I was trying to describe my life in Berkeley, breathlessly rushing toward impossible goals, to that vague "something out there." When I explained how conflicted I was, loving to do certain things and hating others, the women laughed and tried to understand. Finally, Miriam, the grandmother in my Amish family, said:

"Sue, making a batch of vegetable soup, it's not right for the carrot to say I taste better than the peas, or the pea to say I taste better than the cabbage. It takes all the vegetables to make a good soup!"

Miriam's words remind me of the old children's tale called Stone Soup. The tale goes like this:

Before the stranger came, everyone in the small village was hungry.

No one had enough to eat; each person hoarded what little he had. And the peasants feared strangers. One day, an outsider came to stay in the village. A few days later, he began boiling water in a very large pot. He proceeded slowly and carefully to add very large stones, one at a time. Finally, one of the villagers asked what he was doing. "I'm making stone soup," the stranger replied. "It's still missing something, but would you like to try some?" The villager tasted the soup and agreed. Something was still missing.

"Maybe I could go home and bring you a few carrots to add to the soup," the villager offered.

One by one the other villagers came. Each of the villagers tasted the soup and then offered to add to the soup what they could spare. One brought a few potatoes, another an onion, another a cabbage, until there were many rich and varied ingredients in the soup.

As they waited for the soup, the villagers gathered together around the pot, telling each other stories, feeling they were all a part of a wonderful celebration.

That feels like what I've been doing. I've been making a stone soup. Friends — the Amish, Buddhists, those in A.A. and Alanon, those who don't practice prayer in ways that bear a label but who are equally committed to living their prayer — with great generosity, offered their carrots and cabbage and onions and potatoes.

Together we make a good soup.

From all these friends I have learned to pray.

Praying for Power

STELLA TERRILL MANN

$\mathcal{W}$e are always trying to change our lives from what they are to what we want them to be. We are tired of poverty, tired of failure, tired of our old humdrum jobs. We want to leave our feelings of frustration about the present and anxiety about the future behind us. We want to produce more, be more. We want to have more security and more freedom than we ever have known. We want more love, beauty, and peace in our lives. We want what Jesus was talking about — to have life and to have it more abundantly!

Oh, if we only had the power to soar out, up, and away from this drab existence. If only we could wake up tomorrow in a bright new world. If only we had the power. Power? What is power?

According to Webster's dictionary, power is "the ability, whether physical, mental, or moral, to act; the faculty of doing or performing something; capacity for action or performance or for receiving external action or force."

That gives us something to work with. What we really want then, is the *ability to act* and the *ability* to *receive external action* or *force*, which implies that this external action or force may have an effect on us and, possibly, on our beliefs.

Let us start our search for power by first looking into the possibility of receiving an external force that will help us solve our problems.

A little clear thinking brings us to the conclusion that all human beings, whether they are a headhunter in the jungle or a fortune hunter on Wall Street, realize there is an external force or power to which they can appeal for help. Their different methods of approach to this power and their different beliefs about what it is and how to use it vary with the level of intelligence or learning of the individuals. The significant thing is that they *all believe* in this power. They do not all try to call it. But they all know it exists. And when an individual does call on this power for help, he gets it according to his understanding of the power and the amount of his belief in it.

It is my personal conviction that every living thing is aware of this power. I believe all forms of life use it and in most instances obey its dictates without question, and in some instances without the possibility of choice. I think there is no other way we can, for example, explain the perfect flight formation of certain shorebirds or the migration of many birds and animals and the almost human intelligence many of them display as they make their journey. I further believe that it is through this power that we are able to connect with the intelligence of the animals who share our lives. I am sure that in varying degrees this same power lies in every atom in the universe, whether that atom be of gold, flesh, flower, or star.

I further believe that the healing agency in medicine, vitamins, minerals, and the building blocks in calories resides in this power which is inherent in them.

If the birds of the field, the plants of the earth, the stars in their courses, and the waters in their falling know and use this power, cannot you and I also use it? Does not man have dominion over all?

Jesus of Nazareth was a man who knew and used this power, which has ever since been termed Christ power. Where did He get this power? What was it? How did He get the "capacity for action and performance" that we have since termed the miracles? Of what did His capacity for "receiving external action or force" consist and what external action or force came to Him? And why?

We know that Jesus' use of this power proved beyond all doubt that man can control his circumstances instead of being controlled by them. That is what we want to do, is it not? Jesus said that of Himself He could do nothing; that He, the mortal man, the citizen of Nazareth could do nothing and that the Father in Him did the works. Well then, what is the Father? Our Creator, God.

Now we have the secret of it all. The power we want is already ours. It is our share of *God-Mind*. We have a share of ultimate truth, beauty, wisdom, and life — all that God is. It is our ability to create, to hope, to love, to worship, to learn, and to live forever. But how large a portion is our share?

Jesus said there was no limit except that which we ourselves placed upon it. We have as much as we believe in and will call on and use. The power is not outside us, not in the mountain, not in Jerusalem, no, but exactly where Jesus said it was — within us. We do not have to ask or beg for this power. It is already ours, here and now, awaiting our word or direction. It lies there, inactive, until we release it by our words.

"All that the Father hath" is ours, yours, and mine. That is a fact that should send us to our knees in awe and jubilation, if we understand even the smallest part of it. Jesus knew and promised that we could do even greater than He did. I have not the slightest doubt that we will learn and do even more than He did. But long before we have learned even a fraction as much as He knew, we can learn enough to change our lives from what they are to what we want them to be. And the way to learn is by prayer.

Modern science says space is charged with energies (which means power) that would transform the earth, if we knew how to, and could, control them. Jesus said that if we had the faith of a grain of mustard seed we could move mountains. There is only one energy in the universe; one energy in many forms.

And how will we induce this power or energy to move in our behalf? By thinking. On the physical plane we can burn coal and release the energy in it. On the mental place we can use thought to release and direct this one energy of the universe. On the spiritual plane we can release this energy through love and faith.

It comes down to this then: we do not have to create a power. All the power there is or ever will be already exists. We need only learn how to release it, how to direct it to do our bidding. Man has free will. He, like God, can and does create. Nor can he help creating. His every word creates after its kind. His every thought creates. Words and thoughts are commands for this power to act. And it does act, whether our word be a curse or a blessing, or our desire be to destroy or to create.

What we need to learn is how to use this power wisely. We have already learned that, unless we use it for the good of all, we will not have solved our problem but will have created a new and worse one. We want to live, so, we desire bread. But if we murder in order to get the money to buy bread we have not solved our problem but have created a new one. We have to learn to lean not on our own understanding, but to consult God in everything.

What do *you* want? Use the power that Christ used, pay for it and take it! What will it cost you? It will cost you *decision, knowledge, faith,* and *work*. These will release and direct the power that waits to serve you.

You must decide. This is, in effect, placing your order for what you want. It notifies nature that here is one who intends to accomplish. You alone must decide what you want, decide you can get it, decide where and when and how to start, and decide that you will then keep on and on. God Himself cannot give you your heart's desire until you know definitely what it is you do want. Decision releases power and directs it.

Having vague thoughts and wishes about what you want to do with your life will give you no happiness and no success whatsoever. Few people ever know what they really want from life. But those who do know exactly what they want, and want it badly enough, always get it. Because the act of making a decision has the power to open the way to opportunity, to draw strong people to you who can help and to breed success.

After coming to your decision you must take the next step: you must gather knowledge about your desire so that you will know how to go about achieving it and how further to direct the power that is already within you. This is active prayer. Applied knowledge is prayer. It does no good to possess the knowledge unless it is used.

The world is organized for people who know what they want. The world stands ready to help the person who sets out to help himself or to bring about needed reforms that help all men. For all men know what is good and right and Christlike. Many people think they must have money or influence before they can begin a project of mercy or reform. They ascribe too much power to money. If money had as much power as we commonly give it, why do we see rich men's sons who lack even the power to hold on to the fortunes they inherit? If money meant power, then only the wealthy would ever have power, and no poor boy or girl would ever be able to start from the bottom and create a fortune. The truth is the other way around; he who uses the power he has can create a fortune or anything else that he wants.

A thousand hands stretch out to help the one who starts out to help himself and others, for such a one has given notice to the world that he is aware of his power and that he intends to use it. The world loves people who do things and honors those who do them well. And the top performers are handsomely paid. Why not? Our hero worship grows out of a very fine instinct. We are saying that we not only approve of and praise our heroes, but that we do so because we know that we too can do better; and we enjoy living vicariously through the life of our heroes. We admire those who have used their power better than we have used ours. We are grateful to them for silently reminding us of our own inheritance.

Having come to your decision, and gathered information and knowledge about the thing you want to do, you now have to invest your faith in your project.

Some people achieve a state of constant faith by what I term the lump sum method. They accept God as their Creator, themselves as immortal, and the world as a training school in which they cannot fail. They go about the business of asking for and getting answers from God as naturally as they eat or sleep. Opportunities open to them as if by magic. They make friends who go out of their way to help. Talents and abilities that they did not suspect they possessed blossom and grow. They lead a charmed life.

Others find it hard to develop a working faith. If you belong to this group, start with small easy steps so that you may gain faith in accomplishment. Choose and complete a simple act of faith; then try another and another. Every act of faith is added to the total store.

I know a woman who is developing her faith by the step method. For a long time she practiced "setting her mind" so that she would wake up at an exact time every morning. After she became perfect at that she started other tasks. Always she thought in terms of God's doing the work, of turning within to the power that is in direct contact with God-Mind everywhere. This is what Jesus meant when He said that none could go to the Father except through Him (Christ). He did not mean the mortal man Jesus of Nazareth, but the inner soul or mind, which He said we all have.

One day this woman couldn't find a pair of scissors that she badly needed. Before her campaign to develop constant faith she would have spent time and energy blindly looking for them. Now she sat down and quietly realized that there is but one Mind; that her individual mind was connected with it, being a part of it; that anything in God-Mind could be reached by her individual mind, and that the solution to any problem she ever could or would have would be in God-Mind.

After awhile the woman thought to look in the bottom drawer of the linen chest, between the last two sheets. There she found the scissors, where her daughter had apparently misplaced them after using them to cut the string around the laundry bundle before putting away the clean sheets. The woman never would have thought of looking there by the old trial and error method.

The problem was little, but the principle is the same one that moves mountains — the same one that carries you from where you are to where you want to go — to success, service, and happiness. By taking that little step of faith the woman was preparing for the times when she would use her faith to face more important challenges, just as the athlete, as he successfully goes through his paces, draws closer to perfection.

You have come to a decision, gathered knowledge, and generated faith. There then remains the last step: work. That will take time and energy. But you have plenty of both. And, as Dorothea Brande points out in her book *Wake Up and Live* (1936), it also takes time and energy to fail.

How then will you work to achieve your big purpose in life? By doing the first thing first, then the second, and so on, leaving nothing out until you are done. This is prayer without ceasing. Said Josiah Gilbert Holland (1819–1881):

> Heaven is not reached at a single bound;
> But we build the ladder by which we rise
> From the lowly earth to the vaulted skies,
> And we mount to its summit rung by rung.

Step by step, rung by rung! It is just as easy for you to become the highest paid and best man or woman in your chosen work as it is to remain on the bottom rung. As easy? Easier!

It is easier to succeed greatly than it is to fail miserably. Why? Because once you get off that bottom rung, you find less competition, fewer hopeless thoughts, a more encouraging atmosphere, and fewer obstructions in your way. Every time you go up a rung it means smaller crowds and fewer irritations. The higher you go the freer you are to accomplish your goal. Also, as you climb you will find more intelligent people who not only understand what you are trying to do but will help you do it. You will find people who make good instead of making excuses. They are the ones who have discovered that all constructive work, done with the right attitude, is prayer.

There is always more room at the top than there is at any other place on the ladder of success. That is because most people have so little faith in themselves, change their decisions so often, and attempt to accomplish their work with such feeble efforts that they remain on the bottom.

What do you want? Fame? You have all the power in the universe at your disposal to achieve that goal, just as you have all the oxygen you need to breathe. But despite the tremendous power available to you, if you set out merely to win fame and fortune you probably never will get them. That is not how it works. A great voice teacher tells me that when a student comes to him saying, "How soon can I get a radio contract?" or "How soon can I get into the opera?" he does not take that student. He says he has never known even a very talented singer to win success that way. He says the talented ones win success by wanting to sing so much that they take the necessary pains to learn the right technique. They develop the power that is in them. When they do finally learn, he says, their joy in expressing themselves is so immense, their own thrill so tremendous, that they automatically thrill others. The public demands to hear them sing. Fame and fortune have been achieved as a result, not as a goal. To sing beautifully and perfectly was the goal. To ask God to be able to do so was the prayer that made it possible.

This holds true in every walk of life. The person who works only for money never earns as much as the person who loves his work so intensely that if he didn't have to earn a living he would go on doing it for pleasure. That is praying while you work and making your work a prayer.

But if you do want fame there is one infallible way and you already have the power to achieve it. You have but to release that power. The one thing that never fails to lift a human being out of the ordinary class and place him in the "honored of men" class is service to mankind.

Abraham Lincoln was an ordinary man who loved people. He wanted to serve people. What he knew of psychology, statesmanship, and economics came from the Bible. What he knew of the needs of the people came from his heart. He was a man who knew God, and who knew how to pray.

People come to me saying, "Yes, I know my life has been a kind of failure. I haven't done much but just live. I used to think I'd like to do something for humanity, but I'm too old now. Not enough time left." To all who feel this way I say:

"An average lifetime is 70 years. That means 840 months, or 3,640 weeks, or 25,568 days, or 613,632 hours. But that is not all. Every hour has 60 minutes, so in 70 years you have 36,817,920 minutes which is 2,209,075,200 seconds. And it takes only 1 second to get a flash, a new insight into life and living, of possibilities that will change your whole life, and perhaps the whole mode of living for the world, eventually. The trouble is not with time. You have plenty of that. Your trouble is that you do not have a purpose in your heart. You have not come to a decision. Because when you decide on your purpose, your decision becomes a request; and when you are committed to your decision, your decision becomes a prayer. And if you asked and truly wanted to do something, you would have faith and would be willing to wait on the Lord. Nothing keeps you from success but yourself."

Such purposeless people think they can kill time, only to find that wasted time kills them, and kills faith, ambition, and ability. But one earnest desire can bring it all to life again. Always, always, the Father runs to meet us when we become disgusted with our miserable failures and arise and come to Him.

There are other people who come to me saying, "I want to do thus and such, but I am afraid I can't because of my inherited traits and my past or present environment." Then they tell me a long story about how their childhood was ruined and their education neglected and, so, even though they have a desire to do a thing, it would be useless for them to attempt it. In other words, they believe they have a desire but not the power to fulfill it. To these people I say:

"Your inheritance goes back through all your ancestors to Adam, to God. Draw out the good from all of them and discard anything you don't want. Environment means the thoughts you live in and not the house and neighborhood. It means your hopes, and your whole attitude toward life, God, and the universe, and not what your neighbors do or fear or think of you."

I tell them that "Inheritance can give you red hair and a straight nose. Environment can give you habits such as saying 'You all,' or eating with your knife. Inheritance and environment function on the physical and the mental planes, respectively. They are the two lower planes. There is a higher one that overcomes the lower ones. There is a power that, when appealed to, can overcome every handicap of inheritance and environment and enable you to live a happy, useful life and accomplish wonders.

"That power is what I call God's 'guarantee' to the individual. Through no fault of his own, the individual is given certain parents, and is placed, at least for awhile, in a certain family environment — two factors that are beyond his control. If the parents and the household are troubled, it may be said that such a person is born with two strikes against him. But God is fair. His guarantee to the individual reads like this: If you have a *desire* to do a thing, count it as proof positive that you can do it no matter what the obstacles. Desire and fulfillment are two sides of one whole. If it were not possible for you to fulfill the desire, it would not be possible to entertain it either. The desire is God's silent plea to let Him work through you. It is God's silent guarantee that He will see you through if you will but begin."

Yes, my friends, each of us has a work to do. We are not forced to do it. The more sorely we are dissatisfied with our situation in life, the more tormented we are by an urge to do a thing, the more certain it is that God is inviting us to take the step. Always, always, the urge is the silent invitation on the one hand and the guarantee of our success, if we will make the attempt, on the other.

What do *you* want? It is yours for the taking. Ah, my friend, you are immortal! God exists. You have the same power within you that Christ had within Him. Believe it, use it, and you cannot hope too much, nor dare too much. For in Him you live and move — forward, forevermore!

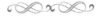

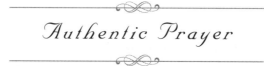

Authentic Prayer

AVERY DULLES, S.J.

*P*rayer is misunderstood when it is practiced as if it were a technique for self-empowerment that is supposed to enhance our psychic powers in some magical way. When prayer is approached in that way, God, if He comes into it at all, is regarded as a means of accomplishing our desires. Prayer, seen in this light, turns God into a means to an end; it instrumentalizes Him and gives undue importance to our own aspirations.

In authentic prayer these priorities are reversed. The decisive matter is God's will, to which we seek to conform ourselves. Prayer therefore has a receptive component in which we try to discern God's will and dispose ourselves to accept it and subject our lives to it. To emphasize God's primacy Jesus taught His disciples in the Lord's Prayer to begin with the petitions, "hallowed be Thy name; Thy kingdom come; Thy will be done. . . ."

The first petition, "hallowed be Thy name," is really an act of adoration. We lovingly prostrate ourselves before God, affirm His absolute goodness, and extol Him for being what He is. The inspired authors of Holy Scripture frequently burst into exclamations of praise, called "doxologies," and the church does likewise in its liturgies. Whether spoken or silent, adoration is true prayer. Some contemplatives devote their whole lives to praise and worship, letting their hearts be carried away, even here on earth, by the beauty and goodness of the divine. This kind of prayer is a hope filled anticipation of the vision of God that the saints enjoy in heaven. By thus magnifying the Lord we fulfill one purpose of our creation, which is to praise and revere our Creator and Redeemer. Our acts of praise often overflow into acts of thanksgiving.

In the second petition we ask, "Thy kingdom come." We look forward to the day when Christ will return in glory to subject all things to His heavenly Father. We joyfully echo the prayer of the early church, "maranatha" — "Come, O Lord!" The coming of the kingdom is realized in a partial and proleptic way by the sending of the Holy Spirit whom the Lord promised to pour out upon all flesh in the "last days" (Acts 2:17) that have begun with Christ's entry into glory. We ask in this petition that the Lord may establish His rule more fully even now, within history, through the Spirit.

Thirdly, we ask, "Thy will be done." This might seem superfluous, since nothing could happen without God's willing it. He is, to be sure, the all-powerful Lord of all things. And yet there is a sense in which sin and evil contradict God's will and grieve the Holy Spirit. God allows evil because He does not want to turn history into a puppet show in which He pulls all the strings. He respects the freedom and autonomy of His creatures even when they deviate from His plans for them.

The prayer that God's will be done is closely linked with other petitions in the Lord's Prayer. In asking to be delivered from temptation and the power of evil we express our longing to serve God better. In asking for the forgiveness of our sins we express our will to be united to God as His friends and to become agents of His peace and reconciliation in the world, forgiving others as we have been forgiven.

One of the most important effects of our prayer is the transformation it brings about in ourselves. To the extent that we are transformed into Christ's own likeness, God can use us better as free, active, living agents in His government of the universe. To contribute to the coming of the kingdom we need more wisdom and prudence than we can gain by our own efforts. By pondering the teachings and example of Christ, and of those who most resemble Him, we obtain the light and inspiration to see better what God may be asking of us. Divine guidance is one of the finest fruits of prayer.

Ignatius of Loyola wrote a book, *The Spiritual Exercises* (1541), that consists primarily of meditations designed to help us find God's will for ourselves. We are urged to contemplate God's activity in nature and history, especially in the sacred history of the Gospels. By immersing ourselves in the great mysteries of our redemption, we can take on Christlike attitudes and discern the changes that are needed in our own lives.

True prayer is never a merely human work. It involves God's activity within us. The Holy Spirit testifies in our hearts that we are God's children and heirs of His kingdom. When we do not know what to ask for or how to do so, the Spirit intercedes for us "with sighs too deep for words" (Romans 8:26). Often enough, we are inspired in prayer to ask for the very thing that God wants to give us — provided that we ask for it.

God invites us to ask not only for spiritual blessings but also for material favors, even such commonplace matters as our daily bread. We ask not only for ourselves but for others as well, since all the petitions in the Lord's Prayer are phrased in the plural. Christians pray with and for one another. To commend others to God's merciful care is itself an act of love. Paul's constant intercession for his young Christian communities provides us with a splendid scriptural model.

As already noted, prayer cannot be an effort on our part to usurp God's dominion. We stand before the Lord not as rulers but as beggars, acknowledging our poverty and unworthiness. Paul asked the Lord three times to be delivered from some illness or affliction, but his petition was not granted. Instead he received the answer, "My grace is sufficient for you." In this way he learned the hard but consoling lesson that God's "power is made perfect in weakness" (2 Corinthians 12:9). The power of prayer differs vastly from what the word "power" usually means to human beings.

At times God comes mightily to the aid of His children, as He did in delivering Peter from captivity under Herod Agrippa (Acts 12:3–11). But very often God allows His children to glorify Him by their suffering and death, as did John the Baptist and, on a later occasion, Peter himself. When Peter conversed with the risen Jesus on the Galilean seashore, he was informed of his destiny to be bound and martyred. When Paul was converted at Damascus, the Lord foretold that he would glorify God by his great sufferings.

Petitionary prayer, therefore, must include the proviso that Jesus added to His own prayer at Gethsemane: "Nevertheless, not as I will, but as Thou wilt" (Matthew 26:39). By this prayer Jesus prepared Himself to drink the chalice the Father had prepared for Him and even, it would seem, to endure a sense of utter abandonment on the cross. If we are unprepared to suffer, we shall never become adept at Christian prayer.

Sometimes Christians give up prayer on the pretext that human beings cannot influence God, who is eternal and changeless. Here we touch on a great mystery. From our limited human point of view we will never be able to comprehend the relationship between time and eternity. But we can be sure of this: that God, in His eternity, knows everything that happens in time. To Him, all things are present. The object of our prayer is not to produce some change in God but to achieve His greater glory in the world and in ourselves. God sees to it that we shall not have prayed in vain.

Can genuine prayers ever be ineffective? Jesus repeatedly assures us that whatever we ask in His name will be done (John 14:13–14; 15:7; 15:16; 16:23). It is certain that God, who is all-powerful, will answer prayers according to His discretion. We sometimes ask amiss. God's wisdom and love are the great safeguard against our selfishness and folly. We must be grateful that God does not let history be controlled by the whims and fancies of His creatures, even creatures who turn to Him in supplication. If we ask humbly, modestly, and with unwavering faith, we shall not be disappointed with God's answers, even when they differ from what we were hoping for. Prayer makes the goodness and power of God available to us, while at the same time it attunes us to His most holy will.

Prayer, then, is far from useless. It brings us into a deep personal relationship with God, foreshadowing in some measure the joyful contemplation of heaven. It enables us to discern God's presence in the events of our lives and to accept what happens to us with loving gratitude. In addition to this passive or receptive effect, prayer changes our conduct and enables us to discover our role in God's plan. By transforming our wills and hearts, prayer gives us new eagerness and power to serve the Lord. In addition, it disposes us so that God can fittingly confer His higher gifts upon us, including, perhaps, the gift of being able to suffer for His glory. Prayer is a human participation in the omnipotence of God. Many good things in history happen because people have prayed and many bad things happen because people have failed to pray as they should.

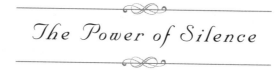

The Power of Silence

BROOKE MEDICINE EAGLE

*A*s I mature to embrace life more fully and openly, I am coming to know it as the great cosmic and universal song my elders have spoken about since time immemorial. This makes it clear to me that prayer is the simple and profound practice of stilling ourselves enough to hear the harmony that reverberates for each of us alone from the great Source of the Song.

In all creation stories, it is told that in the beginning was a chaotic soup of powerful energy. The Great Oneness, who was perhaps bored and a bit lonely being only One, decided to create Diversity within itself — and so a great song was sung, an infinitely complex symphony of sound set in motion that echoes for all eternity. Thus, the Word was spoken — the Song was sung — and all creation began unfolding in its eternal blossoming. Each of us was sung into existence by this same eternal song, and our lives are energized and guided by that unending energy. (Even modern science has finally come to understand this — that all things have their basis in vibration and each is totally unique.)

This has very important implications for us in our daily lives: The gift of life and its unfoldment has already been given — its blossoming assured. A greater and more exquisite plan than we can conceive is moving life forward in beauty.

The most formidable challenge of being human is that we have been given the task of Freedom — the challenge of either choosing to be trusting and open and clear enough to accept and honor Creator's unfolding plan of love and beauty for us, or of creating our own way from the smaller view that we possess as individuals. It has been wonderful to feel the empowerment of our own creativity and choices, even though we have often ended up with less than the best for ourselves. What we have forgotten is that there is great creativity — and ultimate freedom — in quieting our striving enough to tune in to the great Song that created us in the first place, and then to ride the waves of song that are ours alone. We will be kept happily, even joyously, busy picking up that internal song and singing it through our lives into manifestation in the outer world. My people call this Flower Song.

Thus, Everything is present in seed or in bud — already gifted; thus, prayer is not about asking for what we think we want so much as it is silencing our small voice to listen to the Great Voice inside and all around us.

Opening to the silence is an individual task — to hear, to feel the flow of aliveness coming to us in its particular form is ours alone to do. No books, or master teachers, or religious leaders, or friends, or bosses — no one and nothing except our own heart — can hear the tune that is for us alone. How else could we each be guaranteed the guidance that is ours?

The challenge of today is that we have been told the opposite for all our lives, in almost every aspect of our lives, from religion to business. It served those who wished to dominate and use our energy to have us believe that they knew what was best for us. It's pretty silly when you really look at it, but since our nervous systems and brains were literally built to look outward, it is not so easy to release that foolishness.

The first step is awareness. That is why vision quest, retreating, fasting, and all forms of withdrawal from daily life for spiritual introspection are so valuable. They give you the chance to confirm what you already have an inkling of — that your own spirit opens up and gifts you enormously if you only give it the opportunity, the silence.

SILENCE OF THE MIND

The southern seers' way to achieve that silence focuses on the mind as well as the emotions. Thinking and emotions, the ancient ones remind us, are where we tie up the majority of our energy. There are practices from all forms of spirituality that focus on giving us the mind space to touch into the Invisible, rather than continue the chatter that keeps our old ways in place.

Fasts such as vision quests are excellent practice. My elders have taught me that human consciousness likes to be busy: it can be occupied with basic or "level," awareness, with openness to new experience, and with positive intent as readily as with low-level entertainment, re-running old patterns, and negativity. Fasting uses this aspect of our makeup to our advantage, whether we fast from food, TV, our usual daily routine, physical activity, or our old habits.

Traditional vision quests are comprised of several useful parts: The first is the groundwork laid prior to the quest, which includes cleansing the body by eating lightly, practicing the quieting of meditation, and getting our purpose or intent clear. Second is the fasting itself, which includes leaving behind everything but vital necessities like the clothes one wears and what is needed for protection from the elements. Left behind are family and friends, daily routines and employment, familiar surroundings, food, sometimes water, and even physical movement (one is asked to sit, unless doing very specifically prescribed actions of prayer).

The third element then comes: the vacuum created by leaving all this usual activity behind. One soon finds that the real challenge is to create a vacuum in the mind, for in the face of all other inactivity, the mind often goes wild with thoughts, chatter, fear, imaginings, memories, expectations, and so on. You find that you bring your usual life with you via your mind, even though you have done all the outer work of leaving it behind! This is why a previous meditation practice to learn to still the mind is so helpful. Yet it's worth a few days of our time even to discover how strong is this tendency of our mind to carry the old!

Even if our meditative practice has not been developed, there usually comes during a vision fast some precious moments when the mind slips into stillness. Then emerges the gift — the real reason for the quest. Into the vacuum one has created, something must come! The consciousness calls out for something to engage it. And what engages it, but Spirit! The invisible — the more subtle realm that we usually override with our preoccupation with what is "real" and visible — now has a chance to come forward and present itself. Voilà! Vision! We see beyond the veil and perceive the deeper and more universal truths. These are invaluable in our lives.

This kind of questing reinforces, if we are aware of its true process, how invaluable it is to learn to still our minds and to focus our intent on opening to the Invisible in our daily lives. "Leave room for the mystery," my teacher Dawn Boy would exhort me. "Don't fill your life up with all your petty knowing. Leave space for something more mysterious, more beautiful, more magical, more profound, than you can presently even imagine. The Great Creator has more beauty in store for you than you can even dream is possible at this point in your life!"

The basic skill is that of silencing the mind. If there is any one thing I would recommend for you, it is to find a practice that assists you in this. It not only helps you receive information, it helps you receive information that is individual to you. Although everyone is going through this process, each of us has our own needs and our own path. Listening deeply is our personal responsibility. It will serve us profoundly.

One of the important aspects of the silencing is to stop the inner chatter through which we continually create our world. We do our thinking and keep concepts together through language: we do our thinking in words, and we most often express a large part of our emotional experience through words. Seldom do we have pure bodily emotion or a kind of thinking that goes beyond languaging. We put our world together and create the images through which we determine our reality through our internal dialogue. In order for the new to become available to us, we must stop this languaging.

Here is the silencing technique I use. It is based in the southern seer's ways*, and works because it is grounded in our physiology. The focus is on your physical ears, specifically the openings of your ears, so we begin with awakening that part of your body. The process is simple: Place your palms over your ears, in such a way that you create a gentle pressure, a "vacuum seal," so that when you speak you hear it from inside your head, not outside. Now you have effectively sealed your ears. Keep this gentle pressure,

---

*Thanks to Taisha Abelar, *The Sorcerer's Crossing*.

and massage your ears and ear canals by rotating your hands around in circles, forward and back. The next step may take a little practice so that you can accomplish it and keep the seal on your ears. Put your middle finger over your index finger, so you can lift it off and tap your head with a snapping motion. Try this on your knees if you need to — notice that you can give whatever is under your fingers a good strong tap that way. Once you have this down, go back to the position with both your hands sealed over your ears and tap the back of your head — eighteen times.

When you take your palms down from your ears, you may notice a sense of more acute physical hearing. The idea of this is to wake up the sensing of your physical ears and ear canals — to create more awareness there — because this is where your attention must be for the next part of it, the silencing. I even lower my jaw dramatically to open the area around my inner ear from the inside. I suggest closing your eyes as you begin your practice of this, because it cuts down the distractions.

Sit up where you can breathe fully and easily. Begin drawing in full natural breaths through your nose, and as you release your breath, imagine that you can send the air out through your ears! Place the tip of your tongue gently on the roof of your mouth behind your teeth. The final step is to put all of your attention on the openings of your ears, and listen intently. Remember that you want to be able to really feel your ears and ear canals, so if you can't, it might be helpful to actually put your little finger into your ears and give a little massage there to get more in touch with exactly where to put your attention. When you are focusing your attention there, you will not be hearing words inside your head. If you are hearing words, you are not focused on your ears, so return to focusing on them. Put all your attention there. Let any word that comes up be a signal to draw your focus back to your ears.

Practice of this technique, even in conjunction with other

meditation practice, can be very useful. In time you can open your eyes and look around you, yet still not be naming things and talking to yourself about what you see. Eventually, the idea is to move about through your day without constantly naming and categorizing things in your old ways. As Dawn Boy exhorted me, "Leave space for the Great Mystery to offer something new and wonderful!" Everything is unfolding in beauty; we need only stop holding on to the historically and personally familiar.

This inner silence is potent once you can maintain it. Whenever anyone finds true silence, what comes through is what Creator is sending through, unrestricted, and is of very high quality. The definition of the Christ energy, in fact, is one who allows the energy of creation to move through the heart, unrestricted. It means letting go of our control and manipulation to a large extent. When there is nothing else in the pattern, when the "space" is open and clear of all our usual images and beliefs, what comes into the silence is singular and gets all the energy that is coming through, and in this way, manifests immediately! There is an enormous amount of energy available that we normally have tied up in many other ways. This is what the great masters are doing when they literally manifest things like magic! They open to the grace and beauty that Creator planned for them. Nothing clouds the picture — no old ideas, no limitations, no past history, no negativity. It truly is magic, and that is the science of it! What we are doing is stepping into shaman's time, stepping into Creation's blossoming intent, shimmering invisible.

When we act on the side of things made manifest — in the world as we usually know it — the density there requires tremendous amounts of our human energy. Yet this is what we have been trying to do throughout most of our history. We have been attempting to make a difference in our world by pushing and shoving material things around. That has drained not only our personal vitality, but the resources of our Earth. The only way we will truly make a difference at this point is working in a spiritual way; it is our challenge to ourselves to learn this new, magical, graceful, easy way of being, and of doing things. And the key — the basic skill — is silence.

All the external practices we do come to naught if we can't find that place of silence within us. Our connection to our own deep and larger Self lies in the stillness, as does our bond with the great Source of all things, from which comes true wisdom and unerring direction in our lives.

> In the mountain, stillness surges up to explore its own height; in the lake, movement stands still to contemplate its own depth.
> — Rabindranath Tagore, *Fireflies* (1928)

Elder Sara Smith of the Mohawk tribe, Iroquois confederacy, reminds us of her good way: "Meditation is much a part of my being . . . which I now understand as allowing what is so to pour forth from within oneself. It's not from you, but for you. I sit and still myself to allow the answers to come from within, rather than from me dictating what I want and what I think I need."

Since thinking and old emotional patterns tie up a large majority of our energy, these are primary places to focus in freeing up the gift of energy Creator gives us each day. An added wonder and blessing of this gift of continual blossoming is the release and exquisite fragrance for the benefit and unparalleled upliftment of others. Then we truly become conscious co-creators of a beautiful, whole, and holy life for us and All Our Relations.

This essay was adapted from the author's forthcoming book, *The Last Ghost Dance*.

For a complete explanation of Vision Questing, we recommend listening to the author's audio tape, *Visioning*.

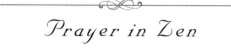

Prayer in Zen

Lou Nordstrom

*T*he Japanese Zen master Soen Nakagawa Roshi once had a student who was an American Jesuit priest. At their first formal interview *(dokusan)* of a seven-day Zen retreat, Soen Roshi gave the Jesuit priest as his *koan,* "What were Jesus Christ's last words on the cross?" The Jesuit priest immediately replied, incredulously but matter-of-factly, "My God, my God, why have You forsaken me?" Soen Roshi promptly rang his bell and said, "No." The priest left disconcerted.

For six days, the priest gave the same response and Soen Roshi each time rejected it. By the seventh day, the priest was completely frustrated and dumbfounded. At the last *dokusan,* he appeared before Soen Roshi pleading with him to reveal the answer that would put him out of his misery. Soen Roshi compassionately complied with the priest's abject request, but in a most startling manner. Suddenly, the priest saw Soen Roshi *become* Jesus Christ on the cross, arms agonizingly outstretched, head thrown back in pure despair, the very embodiment of crucifixion, and heard him howl with the full force of his being — MY GOD, MY GOD, WHY HAVE YOU FORSAKEN ME!

What does this story have to do with prayer in Zen? When this encounter took place in the early 1960s, American Zen had a strongly atheistic cast to it, and many American Zen students would have been appalled at the very *idea* of prayer in Zen. Many — myself included — were zealously attempting to get away from both prayer and God, somewhat mindlessly assuming that prayer is inherently theistic in nature. Soen Roshi would have had a good laugh over this! More than thirty years before so-called "interfaith Zen" would become fashionable, Soen Roshi had opened wide the doors of Zen practice to Western theists, in the spirit of the all-inclusive Way *(Dao)*. Equally iconoclastic for American Zen students was his advocacy of Pure Land *nembutsu* ("name of the Buddha") chanting or mantra recitation practice. He even invented, so to speak, his own mantra, *Namu Dai Bosa* ("Let us be one with the Great Bodhisattva!"), the wholehearted repetition of which he not only endorsed but embodied. For Soen Roshi, there would have been no problem at all using the term prayer in connection with Zen practice. He often spoke of prayer and *zazen* (Zen meditation) as if the true spirit of prayer were no different from that of *zazen*. But, of course, for most of his American students, who by definition "know more" than their teacher, this self-evidently "unZen" idea was just another one of Soen Roshi's charming eccentricities.

If prayer is the experience of what Zen calls no separation of subject and object, self and other, then in that sense there is prayer in Zen. Such prayer would be both objectless and subject-less, however, since in the state of no separation there is neither subject nor object, neither self nor other. Moreover, such prayer would be "empty" — with no separation there is no inherent content or meaning or message. The focus in Zen would be on being one with the act of prayer, or more profoundly Zen would view prayer as the practice of just *being*. Empty prayer would be prayer in a completely all-inclusive sense, since empty prayer is beyond (or prior to) theology, ideology, and sectarianism.

One semantic problem is that traditional "prayer" is not all-inclusive. It usually excludes whatever does not fit the model of God as a separate object of prayer, with a self that prays, existentially speaking, separately from the act or experience itself. This model excludes prayer as non-doing (the Daoist *wu wei*), meaning the state of being one with the act or experience, so that you are not *doing* in the usual, alienated sense.

In addition, there is the problem of stereotyping prayer as primarily or exclusively petitionary — asking for something — rather than what Thomas Merton called "objectless prayer," to which Zen would add *subjectless* as well. This model focuses on the inherent content or meaning of prayer rather than, as in Zen, the direct experience of *being* prayer, the manifestation of *nen,* "this-very-moment mind." Again, Zen prayer would be all-inclusive. Being "this very moment" is a completely open state, devoid of inherent content, meaning, or message.

Soen Roshi was in the same Rinzai Zen lineage as the great eighteenth-century master Hakuin, who is said to have compiled a book of miracles associated with the chanting of the short sutra *Enmei Jukku Kannon Gyo*. When I began Zen practice some thirty years ago, Soen Roshi taught me this sutra. Even though I intellectually rejected the chanting of it as not being Zen practice, I immediately memorized and began chanting it regularly. Thirty years later, the chanting of *Enmei Jukku Kannon Gyo* is still my secret personal practice, the sounds of its syllables as familiar as the sensation of breathing. I do not claim any miracles resulting from its single-minded recitation, but I must confess to thinking of its effect as "magical."

The title can be translated as *Ten-Phrase* (or *Ten-Clause*) *Prolonging-Life Bodhisattva-of-Compassion Scripture*. My own poetic paraphrase would be *The Song of Nen*. Rather than calling it my prayer, I prefer speaking of it as my song. But whether construed as prayer or song, the spirit of *Enmei Jukku Kannon Gyo* is the intense wish for unalienated human experience: *nen*. In the conventional sense of prayer, we pray for this in Zen; or this is what we would pray for if we prayed for anything. Chanting it wholeheartedly is the embodiment of such unalienated experience; being one with this prayer is the granting of the prayer's wish.

Rather than chanting *to* the Bodhisattva of Compassion, *being* this chanting is becoming the Bodhisattva of Compassion; one becomes Kannon of Kanzeon or Kuan Yin simply by being one with this song of no-separation, by being, in the words of Taizan Maezumi Roshi, "most intimate." It is this existential self-intimacy that makes it song, that makes it prayer in the objectless, subjectless sense. Prayer, like song, is about the quality of your intimacy with the direct experience of prayer and song; prayer in Zen is not about what you pray *about*. It is all-inclusive prayer, because aboutness always excludes and separates; content and meaning always divide and alienate.

The Common Ground
of Healing

Paul R. Fleischman, M.D.

$\mathcal{V}$ipassana is an ancient meditation technique that is still practiced today, and that provides an excellent opportunity for helping healing professionals. As a practicing and teaching psychiatrist, I have been aided, through my practice of Vipassana, to deepen my autonomy and self-knowledge at the same time that I have augmented my ability to be a professional anchor to others in the tumult of their lives.

Vipassana touches the common ground of healing. It is acceptable and relevant to healers of diverse disciplines because it is free of dogma, experientially based, and focused on human suffering and relief. It contains the healing element from which the various molecules of our helping professions are built.

What, after all, must we do and be to heal ourselves, and to have energy to heal others? I believe the answer to this question is both obvious and universally acknowledged among healers of differing theoretical orientations. We must see deeply into ourselves, our personal fears and prejudices and conventions and opinions, so that we may stand thoughtfully, clear-sightedly on reality. We must be able to differentiate the accidents of our birth, culture, and particular conditionings from the universal and the timeless truths. We must live balanced, full lives, that sweep up the breadth and depth of what is potential in us as human beings; yet at the same time we must focus with discipline, determination, endurance, and continuity on what is central, essential, critical. We must love, not just those who by accident or choice abut upon our lives, but the potential for awakening that stirs within every life form, so that we can glimpse in the turmoil around us the possibility of an upward-reaching nature. We must accept, bow, acknowledge that death will lead each of us, each of our patients, away, but we must spark faith, hope for this next moment's luminosity in those who are pained, defeated, cynical, withered. We must restrain our own lusts, impulses, needs, yet we must nourish ourselves so that self-containment does not culminate in dryness, but enables the fullness of the fountain of inner life. We must walk the path from ignorance to knowledge, from doubt to clarity, from conviction to discovery. We must start anew every day, without accretions of doctrines and conclusions, life fledglings in the springtime of knowledge.

VIPASSANA IS A WAY

It was discovered twenty-five centuries ago by Gotoma, the Buddha. In the language that he spoke, the meaning of the word *Vipassana* is insight, to see things as they really are. Although Vipassana contains the core of what later has been called

Buddhism, it is not an organized religion, requires no conversion, and is open to students of any faith, nationality, color, or background. In its pure form, which can still be found and followed today, it is a nonsectarian art of living in harmony with the laws of nature. It is the ethical and social path that derives from an exploration of nature within the framework of one's own mind and body. Vipassana's goals are liberation from suffering and spiritual transcendence. It leads to inner peace, which those who practice it learn to share with others. Healing — not the curing of disease, but the essential healing of human suffering — is the purpose of Vipassana.

If *prayer* means linguistic dialogue with a deity, then meditation isn't prayer; but if *prayer* is understood to mean the process of devoted and reverent emptying of self to receive wisdom, then Vipassana meditation is pure prayer.

Vipassana, as handed down from the Buddha through the chain of teachers to U [Mr.] Ba Khin and Mr. S. N. Goenka, has a unique feature among meditation practices, one that makes it particularly relevant to either somatically or psychologically oriented healers. It focuses on the absolute interconnections between mind and body — the subtle sensations that form the life of the body, that continuously condition the mind; these can be experienced directly by disciplined attention. It is this observation-based, self-exploratory journey to the common root of mind and body that shatters dualism and evokes in the student a revolutionary vision of the unconscious origins of the sense of self.

PEACE IS PURITY

The nucleus of inner peace is purity of heart and mind. When you say, "I want inner peace," you mean that you want to be able to live with what's inside you, to be at ease in the depths of yourself, and that integrated positivity, without cracks or seams, is called "purity."

To illustrate what is meant by purity, I'll tell you an experience I had about twenty years ago while my wife and I were young travelers in India. One evening we arrived at a Hindu temple in a steep Himalayan valley through which flowed a tributary of the holy Ganges river. The temple was jammed with salty peasants from the austere uplands of terraced rice paddies, and inside a priest was slowly, methodically, rhythmically smashing a huge bronze gong, which resonated with deafening intensity. We entered and sat on the floor amidst the throng of silenced and transfixed hill-farm families. The gong pulsed so loudly that it shattered our minds, cutting down our thoughts to stubble. This was the evening meditation for the villagers and for the pilgrims who were wandering upward into the sacred mountains. The gong scythed out all troubling thoughts and feelings. Everyone on the temple floor was temporarily relieved of worry, distraction, or confusion, and our minds were of necessity emptied and focused by the monotonic sound. The long day, with its labor, uncertainty, ill-health, quarrels, and bare feet could end in forgetful focus. Anger or dread were driven underground.

The gong's ear-splitting intrusion into our beings dissolved inner tension and layered a zone of mental silence over our lives. This seemed like an understandable way to end a choiceless and chilly autumn day in a poor and rocky life.

This gong illustrated unforgettably the principle underlying many kinds of meditation, including hypnotic drumming or repetition of a mantra. Calm is induced by the repression of mental activity through the creation of one fixed vibration. *Silent* meditation functions differently, with different goals and methods, suited to different individuals or different "karmic" situations.

Where living conditions are more optimistic and there can be more hope for deepened calm, meditation can function in the *opposite* way from meditation with a gong. Meditation without a gong, a mantra, or a mental picture permits distress to rise up, rather than being squelched, and the meditator, instead of inducing a forgetful trance, is mirrored in the silence of his or her own mind. In silent, wordless, imageless meditation, the files of one's own memory, thought, and action are exposed to internal illumination. This sort of meditation can froth with distress that cannot be alleviated merely by driving the demons back underground with amnestic cymbals, but by changing one's entire life. By changing how you live, the residue of your thoughts and feelings as you perceive them in your meditation will be sweetened. Then, what you say, do, think, and feel, when it rises back up in your silent mind, won't need to be staunched. This kind of meditation includes a dialogue, a feedback loop, between active life and meditation, so that life becomes entrained behind awareness and calm. This is what is meant by "purity": cultivating a way of life that you can live with.

Silent meditation isn't a way of forgetting but a way of being unable to forget, an instant replay of your own game. Through silent meditation, we cultivate purity not because we want to avoid hell in some afterlife, but because we want to avoid watching ourselves stumble awkwardly across the internal silent screen. A lifelong commitment to this sort of self-awareness naturally purifies life, deleting whatever is incompatible with silent, tranquil peace. The more rigorously we immerse ourselves in ourselves, the nicer a person we're going to want to be. Purity means being able to relax with who we really are. By this I don't mean mere self-acceptance, but self-transformation, so that wherever we penetrate we find no hindrance or harm. We stop shocking ourselves. Meditation focused on purification isn't something we do to overcome our day, but what we do to guide our day toward sustainable peace of heart.

Inner peace built on purity isn't just psychological; it's a positive circle of action, reflection, and purification: actions that help, purification of states of mind that hurt. When we live with the ramifications of our thoughts, when our view is unsheltered from the effects of our deeds, we will spontaneously want to feel as if light could shine through us from any direction. Deep meditation is built over the realization that what harms us harms others, and that what helps us helps others. Every thought and act that separates us will also bring disharmony in its wake.

Purity is freedom from anger, fear, and passion, the narcissistic emotions. Conversely, love, compassion, sympathetic joy, and equanimity — all pure moments — are boundary-crossers, unifiers, so that purity is always selfless and universal in reach. Purity means egoless, non-self-referential life. Physically, there may be a center of the universe somewhere in the axis of the Milky Way, but meditation reveals that the transformative center of the world will well up inside of us in any pure moment.

A dynamic focus on peace, a selective life, a thoughtful, informed, compassionate and natural life that appreciates the catalytic role of sorrow and the ameliorating beneficence of social service and a realistic perspective, are all spokes on a wheel whose hub is purity of heart. No matter where we start — even if it is opposite to someone else's starting place on the wheel — if peace is our goal, we want to deepen our gong-less purity. Meditation based on purity is exposing rather than soothing, and it elucidates where real, external lifestyle changes can be reflected to shine internally as peace of mind. It is unambiguously ethical. It stresses insight rather than amnesia.

Meditation that focuses on the direct purification of the mind is called Vipassana meditation, and it provides access to the deepest peace. "Vipassana" means "insight" in an ancient Indian language, Pali, in which the Buddha's teaching is preserved, and Vipassana is the meditation technique that the Buddha taught and practiced. Vipassana isn't Buddhism — the organized religion that congealed around the Buddha's teaching after his death — but is a depth psychology, a systematic transmission of objectively observable truths. Although Vipassana has been preserved by the Buddhist community, it is in itself a nonsectarian methodology of self-observation that can be practiced by anyone, regardless of previous religion or lack thereof.

The Buddha himself emphasized that Vipassana was not a discovery unique to him, but a rediscovery of the teaching of all the Buddhas, which can be taken to mean, in a Western historical sense, that Vipassana can be rediscovered by anyone who seeks eternal peace. Elements of Vipassana seemed to well up spontaneously in the lives of Henry Thoreau, John Muir, Mohandas Gandhi, and Rabindranath Tagore, and subtler traces of it can probably be discovered in your own life because it is a natural process. But the specificity of Vipassana as the Buddha taught it shouldn't be confused with the pied personal texture of its fragments within particular people. Elements of Vipassana recur in lives that don't exemplify or complete it. The Buddha's teaching of Vipassana was complete and free of unnecessary extras. Vipassana as the Buddha taught it is exactly and only the path to "nibbana."

Nibbana is unshakable inner peace, absolute purity, that is defined by what it is not: desire, fear, anger. Instead, it is freedom from wish or fantasy, pure reality unimpeded by egocentric blinders. It is insight into the cause of suffering, and release from suffering. The Pali language roots of the word nibbana are variously taken to mean "no arrow," meaning no higher goal to be reached in life, or "no wind," meaning beyond all turmoil and change.

Nibbana can also be defined as the culmination of mental purity, that is the elimination of all contaminating wishes, anxieties, and viewpoints. It is the extinction of craving and aversion, the peace of impersonal perspective, eternal peace realized in this moment.

Cultivation of mental purity to the highest level of perfection is the nibbana the Buddha attained, and the goal of the path he taught. Those peace-seekers of various backgrounds who never heard of Buddha nor nibbana, or who chose different nomenclature for their quest, or who didn't get quite as far, all concur on this quintessential role of purity. When shaggy, wild, unemployed John Muir was wandering in the Sierra wilderness, refusing job offers from Harvard and the Boston Academy of Sciences to ramble in solitude, his goal was not merely to study geology and natural history but to "keep your mind untrammeled and pure." Gandhi declared: "True beauty consists in purity of heart."

Divisive mental states, like self-appropriation, hatred, and anxiety, shatter mental harmony. Those attributes of the mind that are free of negativity and which are affiliative, healing, helping, are called "pure" because they produce both interpersonal bonds and inner peace. What the Nearings cultivated in their garden, what Thoreau reported in his journal, what Tagore lived and sang, were attempts to purify themselves, to unite rather than to divide. The path to nibbana is only a rigorous delineation of common sense: cultivate a peacegiving mind and abandon all that harms us and others.

The laws of nature are simple: the peace of a pure heart comes from doing what helps oneself and others, and from avoiding what harms oneself and others, both in action, and in thought. Ethics and harmony are the same thing.

Purity understood in this way has nothing to do with the moralistic condemnation with which the term has come to be associated in colloquial English, with its historical links to religious intolerance. Purity in the context that Muir and Gandhi understood, and as it is taught in the Vipassana tradition, is less like excision and more like distillation. From real insight into our own well-being, we let go of irritants that we no longer misconstrue as pleasure.

The process of mental purification can be analogized to the skies two nights after the full moon. Darkness has already established its kingdom. Stars mottle the sky. Slowly the moon ascends above the top of the distant pines, casting around and ahead of itself a continuously changing light that enamels the visible world. The spreading sheen absorbs both darkness and individual starlight, until the world is visible in a new light that equally eliminates the golden stars and their black interstices. A single penetrating focus has revealed that in heaven everything can be seen clearly.

This metaphor is very different than that of filth evicted by goodness, or sin expunged by external redemption. Purity is based on the natural process of change. It isn't a consequence of rejection but of neutral, observing light that abolishes nothing but illuminates everything. There is no need to judge and ostracize, the negativity of which would contradict purity itself. Instead, purity expands its presence by a growing glow of insight.

For meditation to actually change lives, and not just be an interlude, it's important to realize that meditation isn't sitting still. It is the cultivation of a permeating perspective. Practiced sitting, it can grow until it accompanies the active mind in its daily tasks. A life of meditation saturates work, family, leisure, and friendship, until the round of existence turns increasingly frictionlessly on the hub of purity and equanimity.

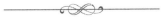

CHAPTER FIVE

"Lord, Teach Us to Pray"

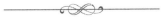

The fewer words the better prayer.

— MARTIN LUTHER

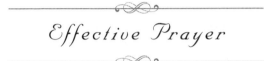

Effective Prayer

BILLY GRAHAM

$\mathcal{F}$ew of us have learned how to develop the power of prayer. We have not yet learned that a man has more strength when he is at prayer than when he is in control of the most powerful military weapons ever developed. I was pleased to hear General Norman Schwarzkopf in an interview with Barbara Walters after the end of the Gulf War say that he prayed for the men in his command.

Effective prayer is offered in faith. From one end of the Bible to the other, we find the record of people whose prayers have been answered — people who turned the tide of history by prayer, men who prayed fervently and whom God answered.

David gave some powerful prayer patterns in his Psalms for those who are going through difficult times.

When you are distressed: "Answer me when I call to you, O my righteous God. *Give me relief from my distress;* be merciful to me and hear my prayer" (Psalm 4:1, italics mine).

When you need mercy: "The Lord has heard my cry for *mercy;* the Lord accepts my prayer" (Psalm 6:9, italics mine).

When you need help: "O Lord my God, I called to you for *help* and you healed me!" (Psalm 30:2, italics mine).

Prayer is powerful, but if our prayers are aimless, meaningless, and mingled with doubt, they will be of little hope to us. Prayer is more than a wish; it is the voice of faith directed to God. One of my favorite verses is: "If any of you lacks wisdom, he should ask God, who gives generously to all without finding fault, and it will be given to him. But when he asks, he must believe and not doubt, because he who doubts is like a wave of the sea, blown and tossed by the wind" (James 1:5-6).

The Bible says, "The prayer of a righteous man is powerful and effective" (James 5:16). Jesus said, "I tell you, whatever you ask for in prayer, believe that you have received it, and it will be yours" (Mark 11:24). I have heard many stories of prayers being answered for a loved one miles away. In *Guideposts* (July 1990), one mother told about a time when she clearly heard one of her daughters cry, "Mom, Mom!" in the middle of the night. But her daughter was a married woman, traveling halfway around the world with her husband. The mother picked up her Bible from the nightstand and went into the family room to pray. She had a real sense of urgency that her daughter needed help. She prayed that God would show her what to do, and then she read Psalm 91 over and over again.

A few weeks later she received a letter from her daughter. This is what had happened. The daughter was in Borneo when she became very sick and feverish. Her husband could not find a good doctor, but after some time located one who took them into his home where he and his housekeeper nursed the woman back to health. The letter ended, "Remember when I was a girl and I would call out, 'Mom,' and you would come rushing down the hall? That night in Borneo, in my fever, I called, 'Mom, Mom'. . . and then I could hear you rushing down the hall."

God sometimes causes us pain so that we may pray for others. Bible teaching, church history, and Christian experience all confirm that prayer does work.

Picture Prayer

JEFFREY BURTON RUSSELL

*P*rayer is action you take in order to realize yourself fully with your neighbors and with God. It is the fulfillment of the great commandment to love God and neighbor. It opens the gate to heaven; heaven is the complete realization of your potential to be who you really are, uniting you in pain and joy with God and with the whole world. Embracing your own alienation and brokenness with honesty and openness is the foundation of prayer; prayer can be choked off by self-will.

Prayer need not be formal. Prayer is anything that you think, say, do, or feel that opens you up and out to love; anything that numbs you to fulfillment in love blocks you from heaven.

If you suppose that prayer is primarily a conscious or formal process, you will become frustrated when you feel uncomfortable with praying or are unable to pray. Formal prayer, whether personal or liturgical, is important, but the core substance of prayer is the motion of your will, and the turning of your character, toward open love of yourself, your neighbors, and God. Conversing, singing, teaching, praying, writing, building, healing, knitting, and making a garden: all are prayer when they are occasions for opening up to love. I could live my whole life in a constant state of prayer if I did not interrupt it with anger, fear, lust, pride, greed, and other obstacles to the free flow of love.

Plenty of negative energy — call it by its true name, "evil" — abides in each of us. To be true to yourself in prayer, you acknowledge this evil in yourself and hand it over to Christ for Him to transform. When you reach out in prayer, He transforms your anger and enmity into forgiveness and your fear, lust, and greed into contrition. For example, when I find myself angrily thinking "you damned idiot!" of myself or someone else, I can turn that negative energy into positive energy such as a conscious prayer for a sick friend. If the evil continues to block me, I can vigorously summon stronger assistance: The prayer "Jesus, help!" is a legitimate demand on the mercy of God. Temptations do not block prayer unless you yield to them, refusing to turn the negative energy over to God but rather choosing to hold on to it, cherish it, and act on it.

The power of evil to delude, corrupt, and even crush, can be tremendous. The most horrible state of being that I have ever experienced was a moderately severe clinical depression that I suffered from for many months. Clinical depression can be treated with medication. But it is not only an illness: a spiritual evil, an annihilating evil, dwells in its heart as well. In the depths of the depression I thought: I have no way out, ever; everything is meaningless; God does not exist or, if He does, He has no interest in me at all. That was despair. And it was false, because Christ was there. The painful ascent from clinical depression was long, but anytime I struck a spark of hope in prayer, Christ kindled a great flame from it, a fire that melted the barrier that depression had erected between me and the living world of trees, sky, people.

People are an essential part of prayer. Prayer is seldom strictly a matter between an individual and God. Christ said, "Whoever says he loves God and loves not his neighbor is a liar." We pray by ourselves, yes, but we also pray with others, perhaps formally and liturgically, perhaps with an intimate soul-friend, or perhaps with a group. In prayer we are surrounded, aided, and embraced by the communion of saints, by all the people who love God, and by the entire cosmos, which is God's creation and God's great love.

There are many modes of prayer. The mode that I have found most powerful is not a traditional one, though it has ancient roots and has been discussed by psychologists, Ann and Barry Ulanov in their book *Primary Speech: A Psychology of Prayer* (1982).

This method of prayer draws upon my conscious awareness and unconscious images to create what I call a picture prayer. Let me explain. My conscious mind thinks rationally and acts practically, but my unconscious mind, which does not think or use words, expresses itself through feelings and tries to communicate these feelings with pictures as in a dream. I say "tries" because the conscious mind often acts like a despot and uses the unconscious mind as a sort of dungeon to which it sends its disturbing thoughts and feelings. The conscious mind sends fear, lust, and anger into the unconscious mind and then blames the unconscious for harboring disturbing feelings. But when God fulfills you, what is fulfilled is not only your conscious mind, but the whole of your being. When you understand that your unconscious mind is a source of beauty, love, and truth illuminated by the Holy Spirit, you see it not as a garbage disposal, into which you scrape your nasty feelings, but as a transmitter of God's truth.

The unconscious mind is a channel of the Holy Spirit; it struggles forcefully and painfully to bring the Spirit's message to the conscious mind. When your conscious mind refuses to listen, it denies an essential part of yourself, and you are distorted and miserable. During my depression, Christ helped me pry open the trap door of the dungeon into which my conscious mind had shoved my monsters. The monsters gradually came out — or were dragged out, and at the end of this long process, the last monster, a tiny comic one, skittered out and my conscious and unconscious minds joined hands in relief, laughter, and joy. Since then, the dungeon image has vanished, replaced by the image of my mind as a shop on a busy street. The conscious mind is out at the front counter minding the customers (the outside world of people and things), while the unconscious mind draws upon the Holy Spirit to contentedly produce the goods in the back of the shop.

When my conscious mind was setting itself up as an idol to be worshipped and using the unconscious mind as a trash can, I had no way to realize who I really am. You cannot be whole by denying part of yourself, by denying the voice of the Holy Spirit within your unconscious mind, which the Spirit loves at least as much as He loves your conscious self. Prayer unites and mends the broken pieces of yourself into the one, beautiful wholeness. Prayer is cure.

The Holy Spirit's presence in the unconscious mind does not produce logic or words, but feelings, which are often expressed in the form of pictures. You open to the Spirit not by struggling, narrowing, or concentrating, but rather by attending, listening, and hearkening.

When you sleep, the Holy Spirit speaks to you in your dreams. My friend Kristine Utterback, Professor of History at the University of Wyoming, says in a paper entitled "Spiritual

Direction," "My dream gives me a clue to the condition of my soul, and it provides an opportunity to hear what God calls me to do, where He wants me to go." Many dreams are trivial and forgettable. But you know — you can feel — when the Spirit has communicated with you through a dream of power. You often dissipate that power by rushing into an awake state and interacting with the outside world. It is better to take the time to remember the dream, to contemplate it and let it reveal its spiritual message.

The more you pray over a dream and remember it, the more levels of meaning it presents to you. Let me illustrate this point with a dream I had recently while I was contemplating an important decision.

Two friends and I were walking at night down a dark country road toward town; the lights of a seaside village were in the distance. To our right loomed a massive cliff. One friend observed, "Look over there: they've been excavating, and they've found the fossil of an animal a hundred million years old. You can still see the bones." I pushed my way over some rough and shadowy ground and, peering into the darkness, I saw the fossil of a huge and ancient beast. Instantaneously back on the road, I saw the animal rise up like a gigantic bison and try to clamber up the cliff. Its struggle was both majestic and pitiful. It scraped and clattered on the hard granite with its hooves, making slow and painful headway, slipping back and struggling upward, trying to reach the top of the cliff. As I watched with awe and pity, I realized that the animal was not trying to reach the cliff top as I had assumed. With relief, I saw that there was a temple set into the mountainside in a cave fronted with green jade. The animal went slowly inside, returning to the earth to rest.

My conscious mind had been fretting over whether to undertake another large and difficult writing project; the Holy Spirit used my dream to say that, at my age, taking on such a project would be painfully arduous and that what I really needed was to rest in a sacred and secure place.

There is another sort of prayer akin to dream or picture prayer. This related type of prayer, which I call guided imaging, takes place at times such as the transition between dreaming and waking when you are in both a conscious and unconscious state. While on the edge of consciousness, you can open yourself to the feelings within you and yield to the Spirit as your guide.

In this semi-conscious state you can reconnect with feelings, such as anxiety or fear, that your conscious mind either represses or expresses indirectly when you are fully awake. To reconnect with these feelings, you must put yourself in the hands of the Spirit with complete honesty and pay attention to the images that arise in your mind while in the semi-conscious state. If an image should occur that you immediately evade or dismiss, you need to come back to it again and again. If the image represents an issue that your conscious mind strongly wants to avoid, your crafty consciousness will lead you on a detour to other, usually more practical, thought or worry: it may even put you to sleep every time the powerful feeling surfaces. You must keep returning to the image. You will use some conscious reasoning and thinking to guide the movement of your mind, but you must at all costs, avoid rationalization.

A variety of images and feelings will pass through your mind. You will know when you come to the right image because your whole being, mind and body, will resonate to it. When the conscious and the unconscious minds join together, you will know it through a simple physical sensation: you will feel your hand unclench or another part of your body relax, and you will rest in relief. If you stay with that image courageously and trustingly, the Spirit will reveal something important to your life. Your whole mind, conscious and unconscious, will recognize it and the dissonance that you have felt within yourself and with God will dwindle away.

Some years ago, in this process of guided imaging, I encountered a terribly disturbing image, which my conscious mind evaded dozen of times; eventually, through persistent prayer and trust in the Spirit I was able to face it. I was kicking a baby to death, and the worst thing was that I was enjoying it. How could I be such a monster? The tactic my conscious mind repeatedly used to block the image was to put me to sleep for a few minutes; on awaking, less unpleasant thoughts were in my mind, but the underlying tension remained. Persistently I prayed myself back into that image. At last, when my conscious mind was worn down into accepting it, I felt a simultaneous rush of relief as I understood that what I wanted to kick to death was not a real baby, but an emotional part of myself that I had outgrown and needed to dismiss if I were to continue to grow in the Spirit.

The unconscious mind thinks in metaphors, allusions, and paradoxes. It is not ruled by reason and often seems to spin or bounce around wildly. Take it in your arms and cherish it; hold it fast with delight in Christ's light; gradually it will grow calm and communicate to your conscious mind what the Holy Spirit wants you to know. By knowing and accepting what is truly in you, without shirking or evading the truth, you open yourself in the warm love of the Spirit to greater and greater love. That is prayer, that is heaven, the state of peaceful forgiveness.

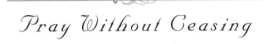

Pray Without Ceasing

JIMMY CARTER

I have posted watchmen on your walls, O Jerusalem;
they will never be silent day or night. You who call on the
Lord, give yourselves no rest, and give Him no rest till He
establishes Jerusalem and makes her the praise of the earth.

— ISAIAH 62:6–7

We all experience rejection. When I was a child, the big boys would choose up baseball teams at recess, and I would often be the last one chosen, because I was small and not a very good athlete. I would have given half my savings from selling boiled peanuts if they would have chosen me as one of the early ones! But being left out, abandoned, or rejected happens to all of us at times. This passage describes the prophet Isaiah's sense that God has forsaken the people of Israel. (Many of the earlier chapters of the Book of Isaiah describe the sins of the Israelites, and the desolation, despair, and suffering they had undergone as a result.) Isaiah's response in this time of tribulation is, perhaps, surprising. He calls on sentinels — watchmen — to sit on the walls of Jerusalem, God's holy city, and offer incessant, constant, repetitive prayer, until the wishes of the Jewish people for reconciliation with God are granted. It reminds me of the apostle Paul's admonition to the early Christians, hundreds of years later: "Pray without ceasing" (1 Thessalonians 5:17).

The message to us is this: Never give up on God, who always answers our prayers. Sometimes the answer is "Wait" or "No," or perhaps, as our pastor, Dan Ariail, says, "You've got to be kidding!" Then we must reassess what we are seeking. Continuing to pray hopefully in the face of profound disappointment seems contrary to human nature. Why should we do it? Because invariably we can learn and grow in the process.

One of the most humorous stories of Jesus was about the woman who irritated an unjust judge so persistently, even at his home at night, that he finally made a proper ruling (Luke 18:1–7). In another story, immediately following the Lord's Prayer, Jesus told of a man who had an unexpected guest and went to a neighbor's house to borrow some bread. The neighbor shouted, "Do not bother me: the door is locked and my children are with me in bed; I cannot get up and give you anything." The man persisted, and got the bread (Luke 11:5–8).

We often find that our prayers bring about change, at least in ourselves, as God opens our eyes to a better future than we could have envisioned for ourselves. The Bible assures us that, with patience and courage, problems, failures, even tragedies can be turned into great blessings. In fact, James tells us, "Consider it pure joy, my brothers, whenever you face trials of many kinds. . . . Blessed are those who persevere under trial, because when they have stood the test, they will receive the crown of life that God has promised to those who love him" (James 1:2, 12).

As we pray continually, even during times when God seems distant and prayer feels fruitless, we immerse ourselves in the benevolence, grace, forgiveness, and love of God. Our attitudes toward life are modified accordingly. This doesn't mean that we become passive or weak. Living in harmony with the omnipotent God makes us stronger, just as seeing the world through the eyes of the omniscient God makes us wiser. And with this new strength comes an increased ability to apply in our lives the blessings given us by God, even in times of rejection, failure, or sorrow. Like Isaiah, we need to maintain our confidence in God's stead-fastness, even in times of loneliness and apparent rejection, and constant prayer is one of the best ways to both express and nurture this confidence.

Communicating our questions, hopes, and fears in prayer makes them — even to ourselves — more open and clear; and the stronger the ties that bind us to God, the more likely we are to live, react, and behave in harmony with exalted standards — and with greater joy, peace, and happiness.

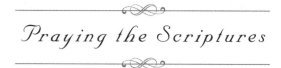

Praying the Scriptures

DALLAS WILLARD

Therefore the Scriptures should only be read in an attitude of prayer, trusting to the inward working of the Holy Spirit to make their truths a living reality within us.

— WILLIAM LAW, THE POWER OF THE SPIRIT (1761)

*T*here is a simple technique that all believers, no matter how trained or untrained, can use to bring to life the spirit and wisdom contained in the Scriptures. It is a practice very similar to the one described by Madame Guyon in the modern edition of her book, *Experiencing the Depths of Jesus Christ*, which was first published in 1688 in Lyons, France under the title *Short and Very Easy Way of Prayer*. (You will find it very useful to read the first four chapters of her book as a supplement to what I am about to say.)

When we come to the Scriptures as a part of our conscious strategy to cooperate with God for full redemption of our life, we must first desire that His will in all things revealed in Scripture should be true for us. Then, we select for study the parts of the

Scripture with which we have some familiarity, such as the Twenty-third Psalm, the Lord's Prayer, the Sermon on the Mount, 1 Corinthians 13, or Romans 8.

You may think that this is not a serious way to begin. But keep in mind that your aim is not to become a scholar or to impress others with your knowledge of the Bible. Seeking to make an impression with your biblical knowledge will only cultivate pride and foster the petty, quarrelsome spirit so regrettably, yet commonly, observed in some who identify themselves as "serious" students of the Scriptures.

These words of Thomas à Kempis (1380–1471) from his *The Imitation of Christ* will help you to avoid that trap:

> Of what use is it to discourse learnedly on the Trinity, if you lack humility and therefore displease the Trinity? Lofty words do not make a man just or holy; but a good life makes him dear to God. I would far rather feel contrition than be able to define it. If you knew the whole Bible by heart, and all the teachings of the philosophers, how would this help you without the grace and love of God?

Your aim must be only to nourish your soul with God's Word. So, go to those parts of the Bible that you already know, and trust your later spiritual growth and study to lead you to other parts as you need them.

In addition, contemplate the meaning of the passages you have selected. As Madame Guyon wisely counsels: "If you read quickly, it will benefit you little. You will be like a bee that merely skims the surface of a flower. Instead, in this new way of reading with prayer, you must become as the bee who penetrates into the depths of the flower. You plunge deeply within to remove its deepest nectar." You may have been told that it is good to read the Bible through every year and to reach this goal you must read a given number of verses per day from the Old and New Testaments. If you do this you may gain a reputation as someone who has studied the Bible and you may congratulate yourself on your accomplishment. But will this practice make you more like Christ and fill you with the life of God?

It is a proven fact that many who read the Bible as though they are taking medicine or exercising on a schedule do not advance spiritually. It is better in one year to have ten good verses transferred *into the substance of our lives* than to have every word of the Bible flash before our eyes. Always remember that "the letter killeth, but the spirit giveth life" (2 Corinthians 3:6). We read the Scriptures to open ourselves to the Spirit.

Come to your chosen passages as you would to a holy meeting with God. Read a small part of the selected passage and dwell on each of its parts, praying for the assistance of God's Spirit in bringing the realities expressed *fully* before your mind and into your life. Always ask: What is my life like because this is true? and How shall I speak and act because of this? You may wish to turn the passage into a prayer of praise or of request.

Perhaps you are reading the great "God is love" passage from 1 John 4. You find it written that "there is no fear in love; but perfect love casts out fear, because fear involves punishment, and the one who fears is not perfected in love" (verse 18).

As you read, you dwell on the ways in which love — from God to us, from us to Him, and between people on earth — pushes fear out of all relationships. You think of the fearless child protected by loving parents, or of how loving neighbors give us confidence and assuage our anxieties. You contemplate how assurance of God's love given to us through the death of His Son suggests that we will never be beyond His care. You then seek divine help in comprehending this and in realizing what your fear-free life might be like. Then you lift your heart in joyful praise as you realize the blessings of living in God's Kingdom. God's Word now speaking *in you*, not just *at you*, creates the faith that expresses God's love *for you*.

Or perhaps we read "The Lord is my shepherd; I shall not want" (Psalm 23:1). At first, we may not automatically transfer this information to ourselves. We may say, "This was true for David, the psalmist." But as we dwell prayerfully on the information there arises a *yearning* that it might also be true for *us*. We can express our yearning like this: "I wish the Lord were my shepherd, that the great God would have for me that care and attention the shepherd has for his sheep!" And as we meditate on the psalm, a feeling of *affirmation* may arise, as it has for so many people: "It must be so! I will have it to be so!" Then we may be moved to express an *invocation:* "Lord, make it so for me." And then we may feel *appropriation* — the settled conviction that it is so and that the words "The Lord is my shepherd; I shall not want" is a statement of fact.

Do not hurry. Don't dabble in spirituality. Give time for each stage of scriptural prayer to play itself out fully in your heart. Remember, this is not something you are doing by yourself. *Watch* and pray.

Now practice the same type of process with those great passages from Romans 8, beginning with verse 28, that begins "All things work together for good to them that love God, to them who are the called according to his purpose" and culminates in a declaration of triumph that no matter what befalls us "we are more than conquerors through him that loved us" (verse 37).

The general process of praying through contemplation of the Scriptures is:

1. *Information* with *longing* for it to be so;

2. *Affirmation* that it *must* be so;

3. *Invocation* to God to make it so; and finally,

4. *Appropriation* by God's grace of its being so.

This last stage must not be forced or, especially, faked. The ability for it will be given to you, as you watch for God to move in your life.

When our minds find inner agreement with the truth expressed in the passages, we embrace the mind of Christ as *our own,* for these great Scriptural truths are the very things Jesus believed. These truths constitute the faith, hope, and love in which He lived. And as they become ours, His mind becomes our mind. Then we become true co-laborers with God, as brothers, sisters, and friends of Jesus in the present and coming Kingdom of God. We can then know and understand in its fullness the *guidance* God gives to His children.

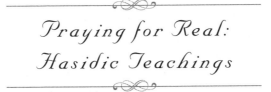

Praying for Real: Hasidic Teachings

YITZHAK BUXBAUM

𝓜ost traditional Jewish prayer (called *davvening*) is ordained: three times a day, or four, counting the bedtime prayers. A person recites the prescribed prayers that are written down in the prayer book. But the question is whether he or she recites them for real or by rote.

Prayer can and should be a pillar in the life of any believing Jew — or Christian or Muslim. But only a solid and strong pillar holds up the roof. If a person prays by rote, he should not be surprised that he finds no life-giving quality in prayer, or that the roof falls in on his religiosity.

How can a person learn to pray for real? Perhaps Hasidism,

which is a pietistic, mystic branch of Judaism that began in the eighteenth century, can provide us with some help.

Praying versus Torah Study

Torah study is usually emphasized more than prayer in traditional Judaism. But because prayer involves more of a direct face-to-face relation to God than Torah study, it was originally emphasized by the Hasidim, who sought an immediate experience of the Divine Presence. The Baal Shem Tov, the founder of Hasidism, devoted great efforts to prayer, and said that he was told from heaven that he attained his exalted spiritual level not because of Torah study, but because he prayed with fiery intensity. Another reason why the Hasidim preferred prayer was because of its egalitarian nature: while not everyone can be a Torah scholar, even a simple person can pray fervently and experience God's closeness.

The Difficulty of Prayer

Prayer is superior, in a sense, to Torah study in helping a person establish a direct relation to God. But perhaps because real prayer is so potent, it is also very difficult, even more so than Torah Study — at least for our generation. Talmud study, for example, may be intellectually difficult, but prayer is emotionally difficult; it demands the service and labor of the heart. Most people find Torah study easier than prayer. Most Jews naturally like to learn, and they find it much easier to exercise their minds than to work with their emotions. Rote *davvening* may indeed be relatively easy. In real *davvening*, however, you have to pass beyond a mere recitation of the words to establish an actual living relationship with God. That is why real prayer will always include personal conversation with God, including petitions, expressions of gratitude, and other additions to the prescribed prayers.

Moreover, in prayer you not only have to face God, you also have to face *yourself*— what your true desires are, what your true spiritual situation is — and that makes most of us uncomfortable. It is agonizingly hard to do. Nevertheless, as the rabbis say about religion and spirituality in general: According to the painstaking is the reward.

REVIVALS

The praying in synagogues today often lacks vitality. That is nothing new; in fact, it is probably the normal situation. But there are sporadic periods of revival when people strive for real prayer and seek to break through the shell of the forms to reach the living content. One such revival was instigated by the Baal Shem Tov, whose Hasidic movement worked to elevate the status of prayer.

A famous story says the Baal Shem Tov once stopped at the door of a synagogue, saying he could not enter because it was so full of prayers. When his astonished disciples asked him if that was not the best recommendation for a synagogue, he answered that when prayers are said with sincerity, they ascend to heaven — but here, since they were said by rote, they did not ascend and entirely filled the synagogue; there was no room for him to enter!

Even today, people find it difficult to enter some synagogues for this reason. They come to the synagogue, stick their head in, and, sensing the lack of real prayer, leave.

But, in the early days of the movement, when the Hasidim found the synagogues spiritually stifling and the prayer services dull and rote, they broke away to create their own vibrant houses of worship. Everything possible was done to inject new life into prayer. Sincerity and spirituality were the keys. The vain musical performances of the cantors were replaced with services led by learned laymen or the Hasidic spiritual masters themselves. Preparation for prayer and inwardness were stressed.

Sometimes the prayers were even delayed until appropriate inwardness was achieved.

THE PARABLE OF THE KING'S ORCHESTRA

The following Hasidic parable provides valuable insight into the process by which this prayer revival occurred:

There was once a king who so loved music that he directed his musicians to play for him each morning. The musicians came to the palace and performed, not only to obey the king's command, but also because they loved and respected the king and valued their chance to be in his presence. So every morning they played for the king with enthusiasm and delight. For many years all went well. The musicians enjoyed playing each morning for the king, and the king enjoyed listening to their music.

When, at last, the musicians died, their sons sought to take their places. But, alas, they had neither mastered the musical art of their fathers nor had they kept their instruments in proper condition. Worse still, the sons did not love the king as did their fathers. They just blindly followed their fathers' custom of arriving each morning at the palace to perform. But the harsh sounds of their music were so offensive to the king's ear that after a time he ceased listening.

Then, several of the young musicians developed a renewed love and reverence for the king, however pale compared to the love and reverence of their fathers, and they realized that the king had stopped listening to their uninspired music. Although they wanted to perform to honor the king, the small group recognized that their inadequate skills made them unworthy to play before him.

So they set about the difficult task of relearning the forgotten art that should have been their inheritance from their fathers. Every day, before coming to the king, they spent time tuning their instruments. Upon entering the palace concert room and hearing the racket of the other musicians, they sought out an obscure corner for themselves where they could play undisturbed. They also remained long after the other musicians had departed, so that they might improve their skill. And in their homes they continued to practice and to struggle with their instruments as best they could.

The king was aware of their efforts and was pleased, for even though they did not play with the same talent as their fathers, still they strove, to the best of their abilities, to once more bring pleasure and joy to the king. Thus was their music received by the king with favor.

This beautiful parable is from the great Hasidic spiritual master, Rabbi Levi Yitzhak of Berditchev, who was one of the early heroes of Hasidic prayer. He used to rise well before dawn to prepare for *davvening*, and was renowned for his ecstatic prayer. Our situation today is not very different from what he describes in the parable. But do we have the determination to "relearn the art" of prayer? In the parable, prayer is compared to making music and the congregation to an orchestra. Everyone knows the extraordinary effort people will make to learn a musical instrument. But do people exert themselves to learn how to pray? Indeed, few people realize that there is anything to learn. When a newcomer, unfamiliar with prayer, arrives at a synagogue, most likely someone will simply put a prayer book in his or her hand, as if to say: Prayer is easy — one just mouths these words! It is as if, when a person walked into a music school, he was given an instrument and told: You just play it. Blow in the end or strum those strings!

THE PARABLE OF THE MAGIC WALLS

Although there are many traditional Jewish spiritual practices for prayer, learning how to *davven* is not just learning a "skill." Even playing a musical instrument requires soul, not just technique — how much more so does praying! Let us consider one aspect of Hasidic prayer as taught by the Baal Shem Tov, who said that real *davvening* must be filled with the fiery intensity of self-sacrifice. He taught that all our activities must be directed to attaining *d'vekut* (a constant, loving awareness of the Divine Presence) and that prayer is particularly effective in achieving this. In the body of teachings of every great religious leader there are always a few sayings or parables that powerfully express what is most basic in his insight. There is one parable by the Baal Shem Tov that contains the very essence of Hasidic mysticism and most poignantly illustrates his teaching about the quest for *d'vekut*. I call this "The Parable of the Magic Walls." Significantly, he sometimes used this parable specifically with regard to prayer, and often told it before the shofar blowing on Yom Kippur:

A king, by magic, surrounded his palace with many walls. Then he hid himself within the palace. The formidable walls were arranged in concentric circles, one inside the other, and they grew increasingly thicker as one approached the center. They had fortified battlements that were manned by fierce soldiers while wild animals — lions and bears — ran loose below the walls. All this was done so that not all who desired to approach would be allowed to do as they pleased.

The king then had proclamations sent throughout the kingdom saying that whoever came to see him in his palace would be richly rewarded; he would be given a rank second to none in the king's service. Who would not desire this? But when many people came and saw the outer wall's awesome size and the terrifying soldiers and wild animals, most were afraid and turned back. There were some, however, who succeeded in scaling the first wall and fighting past the soldiers and animals, but then the second wall loomed before their eyes, even more imposing than the first, and its guards even more terrible. Upon seeing that, many others turned back.

Moreover, the king had appointed servants to stand behind the walls to give money and precious stones to whoever got beyond each wall. Those who had crossed one or a few walls soon found themselves very rich and were satisfied with what they had gained from their efforts; so they, too, turned back. For one reason or another, either from fear at the increasing obstacles or satisfaction with the accumulated rewards, none reached the king.

Except for the king's son. He had only one desire: to see the face of his beloved father. When he came and saw the walls, soldiers, and wild animals, he was astonished. He could not understand how his dear father could hide himself behind all these terrifying barriers and obstacles. "How can I ever reach him?" he thought. Then he began to weep, and cried out, "Father, Father, have compassion on me; don't keep me away from you!" His longing was so intense that he had no interest in any rewards; indeed he was willing to risk his life to attain his goal. By the courage of his broken heart, which burned to see his father, he ran forward with reckless abandon and self-sacrifice; he scaled one wall and then another, and fought past soldiers and wild animals. After crossing the walls, he was offered money and jewels, but he threw them down in disgust. His only desire was to see his father. Again and again he called out to him.

His father, the king, hearing his son's pathetic cries and seeing his total self-sacrifice, suddenly, instantaneously removed the walls and other obstacles. In a moment they vanished as if they had never existed. Then his son saw that there were no walls, soldiers, or animals. His father, the king, was right before him, sitting on his majestic throne while multitudes of servants stood near to serve him and choirs sang his praises. Gardens and orchards surrounded the palace on all sides. And the whole earth shone from the king's glory. Everything was tranquil, and there was nothing bad or terrible at all.

Then the son realized that the walls and obstacles were a magical illusion, and that his father, the king, had never really been hidden or concealed, but was with him all the time. It was all just a test to see who truly loved the king.*

The simple meaning of this profound parable is that we are always in God's presence. The "walls" that seem to separate us from Him are illusory; if we don't see Him, if we don't have the Divine Vision of the Godliness of all reality, it is because of our own spiritual deficiencies. However, the lesson in the story is that if we single-mindedly seek our Father in Heaven, we will find Him. As the son in the parable succeeds in reaching his father because his love overcomes his fear, so must we increase our love of God until all the barriers between us and Him fall away.

Once, when I was discouraged about my own lack of spiritual progress, I asked my own teacher and master, Rabbi Shlomo Carlebach, how one can achieve spiritual growth. He said that the person who is most desperate is the one who gets somewhere.

There is a Hindu story about a disciple who posed this same question to his guru. The guru took him to a river and asked him to immerse himself. When he did so, the guru held his head under water until his lungs almost burst. When he let him up, the guru told him that when he wanted God as much as he wanted that breath of air, he would find Him.

In the Baal Shem Tov's parable, the son's forlorn cries of

---

*In *Sefer Baal Shem Tov* (1968), there are eight versions of this parable. My version is a composite.

"Father, Father!" represent prayer. His readiness to die in his quest not only shows the important role self-sacrifice plays in spiritual growth — but also in prayer. The Hasidic way of prayer, founded by the Baal Shem Tov, is to pray with complete self-sacrifice and with a willingness to give up your life to God in prayer. He taught that before you pray, you should consider that, because of your intense *kavvanah* (God-directed intention), you may die during the prayer, and affirm your willingness to do so. You should say to yourself: "Why should I have any pride or egoism in this prayer, seeing that I'm prepared even to die after two or three words?" He said that the *kavvanah* of some who prayed in this manner was so great, that sometimes, according to the natural course of events, it would be expected that they would die after saying only a few words before God. (Certainly he was talking about himself also!) It was only God's compassion that allowed a person who prayed like this to utter a whole prayer and remain alive. If you are willing to die for each word as you pray, said the Baal Shem Tov, then you must have intense concentration on each word of the prayer. He said that every word has meaning in its own right, and you must put all your energy into saying it.

One of the early Hasidic spiritual masters most famous for praying with self-sacrifice was Rabbi Uri of Strelisk. He once specifically asked someone to do an errand for him, before he prayed, not after, saying: "I'm going to pray now with the intention of giving up my life during the prayer, and I don't know if I'll return again to my home." He wanted this errand done, but did not know if he would live to take care of it later. His son reported that every day before the Morning Prayers his father would go to the kitchen to say good-bye to his wife and children because he did not know if he would die during the prayers from his great *d'vekut* with the Creator.

RABBI ARELE

In more modern times, Rabbi Arele Roth of Jerusalem, who founded a new Hasidic group in the last generation, revived the Baal Shem Tov's fiery way in prayer. I had always found Rabbi Uri of Strelisk's radical teachings, and the vivid stories about him fascinating; but I never understood the matter on a deep enough level to make personal and practical use of it until I read about Rabbi Arele. His experiences and teachings made this Hasidic way of prayer with self-sacrifice come alive for me.*

At a certain point in his life (while still a young man) Rabbi Arele lost the sweetness he had always felt in prayer. His prayer lost its vitality and he became depressed and aggrieved by his woeful situation. In his search for spiritual support, Rabbi Arele read the Hasidic teachings about how one must pray at length, with a loud voice and all one's energy, with *kavvanah* and self-sacrifice. He read how the Baal Shem Tov himself had reached his own high spiritual level by praying with strenuous exertion, with actual self-sacrifice and the willingness to give up his life. Then he tells of a turning point, when he remembered his former days of spiritual happiness, and he felt such bitterness that he thought: "Why should I continue to live any more if this is my lot, to be like an ox eating grass, without a true service of prayer, without holy vitality?" So he decided that he would pray with such self-sacrifice that his soul would depart in prayer, for his life no longer meant anything to him without true service to God. He prayed with tremendous exertion and when he felt himself near death, God had pity on him: suddenly he was bathed in a divine light, almost like that of the World-to-Come, beyond anything he had ever experienced before, even in the good days.

When Rabbi Arele followed the Baal Shem Tov's teachings

---

*The following material about Rabbi Arele is taken from *Toldot Aharon* (1989).

about prayer with utter devotion and self-sacrifice, he reached the mystic goal as described in "The Parable of the Magic Walls." He saw the light of the Divine Presence everywhere and saw how all existence is alive with divine vitality. Rabbi Arele made explicit the promise in the parable. He said that this mystical revelation of the divine light is available to anyone who desires it; even a completely wicked person, who exerts himself over an extended period of time, without giving up, will eventually achieve it. When he reflected upon his own extraordinary experience, Rabbi Arele came to understand that there is no concealment of God; it is simply that the Holy One wants a person to fully exert himself before Him; and when he does, then He will show him mercy.

According to Rabbi Arele, the proper attitude for prayer is to be like a submissive laborer or a simple workman before God, like a hewer of wood or a drawer of water, without any special wisdom at all and without any falseness or crooked cleverness. Prayer requires not only *kavvanah*, but exertion. You can learn this kind of exertion, he said, from someone who chops wood for a living. Regardless of whether the day is hot or cold, the woodcutter won't tire at his hard labor, because he knows that his livelihood depends on it. So when you pray, you should consider yourself to be like a simple woodcutter before God, and resolve to pray with *kavvanah* and bodily exertion, knowing that your spiritual life depends on it.

Just as the early Hasidim broke away to create their own congregations, Rabbi Arele formed a new group to carry out his ideals about prayer. In Rabbi Arele's synagogue, the congregation prayed with the most strenuous and animated exertions. During the time of prayer the whole synagogue was burning with awesome fervor and the clothes of all present would become wet with perspiration from their vigorous exertions in prayer.

The ultimate goal in this kind of self-sacrificing prayer is to fulfill the saying of the Sages: "How much energy should we put into our prayers? So much that we squeeze out our soul [from our body]." When you pray with total self-sacrifice, you reach a state where you are removed from bodily awareness and materiality. Your soul leaves the body and enters the soul world. That is how you achieve *d'vekut* with the Soul of all souls, the Holy One, and achieve the mystical Divine Vision.

We may not all reach the ultimate goal, but we should not be afraid to try; only the holy few will be able to actually risk death to achieve the highest spiritual aims. But we can all take a few steps forward by spiritually renewing our prayers. When we prepare for prayer, we can inspire ourselves by considering how our spiritual life hangs in the balance. We can say to ourselves, "I'm going to exert myself like a simple woodcutter, for I know that my spiritual life depends on this prayer. And if I don't achieve the spiritual purpose of my life, why should I continue to live?" We can also think of the great holy people — such as the Baal Shem Tov, Rabbi Uri of Strelisk, and Rabbi Arele — and inspire ourselves by reflecting on their self-sacrifice in prayer. Perhaps that will help us to pray sincerely and reach our goal of meeting the One and Only One.

The Family and Prayer

HAZEN G. WERNER

There is no place where praying is more appropriate than in the home. Korean Christians have a very wonderful custom in regard to prayer. Upon entering the home of a friend, a Korean will sit down quietly and, bowing his or her head, silently pray for that home. What a wonderful practice!

When we pray with our families, we too can intercede for others: the uncle who is in the hospital, the son who is away in service, the church and the minister, or missionaries in Rhodesia. Remember the people outside your home in your prayer. These words from a mealtime prayer could well be used in our family prayers: "And make us ever mindful of the needs of others." In your family prayer reach out to the peoples of the earth.

The home is a natural center for prayer. What greater thing can the church do than to enroll families in a family prayer movement? John Wesley originated the "class meeting." People gathered together every week for the spiritual renewal that came about through their communal fellowship with God. Family prayer can become the modern version of the Wesleyan class meeting.

As a family, talk to God about your lives; pray about what is happening in your home, about common problems such as jealousy, selfishness, or belittling criticism. Bring the insolubles of your family life to God in prayer. Prayer tightens the family bond and makes it stronger.

Special days, such as birthdays, New Year's Eve, Thanksgiving morning, when the baby is born, when father begins a new job, or when a child starts out to school for the first time, can all become occasions for prayer that strengthens the family and draws everyone closer together.

It is important that children grow up feeling that prayer is a normal part of living. Praying together as a family will, more than anything else, teach a child what it means to live a prayer life. Praying in the home is more important than teaching about prayer in the church school. If there is no praying in the home, a child can conclude that prayer is something that is done only in formal worship on Sunday by a professional religious leader.

Even saying grace before meals can be an opportunity for family prayer. To avoid turning grace into a stilted prayer, let all of the members of the family take part and, at times, join hands and engage in silent prayer together.

Whatever materials, guides, or devotional booklets are used in family prayer, make certain that the praying experience fosters the yielding of the self to Christ and the giving of thanks to God. Each day the family needs to be strengthened; each member needs to recommit his life to Christ and reaffirm his faith. These are the unforgettable and character-shaping experiences that result from praying as a family.

The family should also affirm God in its praying, and thank Him for the priceless gift of being together. If American families would thank God for what they do have, their blessings would grow. Our hearts cannot learn if we lose touch with our gratitude for all of God's gifts. If our hearts are closed, we can no longer see and know the mysteries of His abiding grace in our lives and in our home. Be thankful to God for His enduring love, the wonder of His unending trust, and the joy of His understanding. Affirm God, thank Him, acknowledge Him, and acclaim Him, and your home will always shine with His light.

Young couples who are just beginning their married life can establish the tradition of family prayer by praying out loud together. This is a way of consciously cleansing, healing, and renewing their marriage vows, as well as a way of strengthening the deep and abiding mystic feelings they have for each other. Marriages get shoved about, mixed up, and worn down. There is therapy for all of this in prayer. When you pray audibly together, you are changed. How can you ask God's forgiveness without asking forgiveness of each other? How can you pledge your love to God if you are in a state of bickering and hostility? How can you ask God to hear your plea unless you break the silence following a quarrel, unless you are willing to listen to what your wife or husband has to say? Pray together, preferably at the end of the day.

When you are praying you know God is near. That nearness is made plain to us in this anonymous evening prayer:

'Ere we close our eyes in sleep we would remember before Thee our absent ones. Guard them from temptation and surprise for Thou art in every place. In their weariness, give refreshment, sleep, and rest, and when solitariness laboureth the heart, do Thou breathe a tender remembrance of our love and expectation. O Thou, who art the author and giver of love, enfold them with us in Thine everlasting arms. Through Jesus Christ, our Lord. Amen.

Prayer not only keeps families together; prayer also keeps families living at their best.

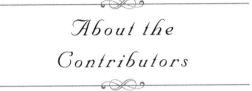

About the
Contributors

FRANCES H. BACHELDER, lifelong pianist and Sunday school teacher for fifteen years, studied at the University of Massachusetts and Purdue University. She now resides in San Diego, California, and, while continuing her interest in piano, also writes poetry and nonfiction. She is the author of essays on Barbara Pym and Anne Tyler and of the book *Mary Roberts Rinehart: Mistress of Mystery*. Currently she is completing her first novel, *The Iron Gate*.

MARK R. BANSCHICK, M.D. is a child and adolescent psychiatrist in full-time private practice. He is a lecturer in the area of child development and the psychology of spirituality and an adjunct professor at Hebrew Union College, New York, where he teaches in the Doctor of Ministry program. Dr. Banschick also serves as an officer for the Mesorah Society, a national organization of traditional Jewish psychiatrists.

Formerly a teacher and family therapist, SUE BENDER is now a ceramic artist, bestselling author, and much sought-after lecturer nationwide. She holds a B.A. from Simmons College, an M.A. from the Harvard University School of Education, and a Master's in Social Work from the University of California at Berkeley. During her active years as a family therapist, Bender was founder and director of CHOICE: The Institute of the Middle Years. Bender is the author of *Plain and Simple: A Woman's Journey to the Amish*, a *New York Times* bestseller with over 400,000 copies sold, which describes her experiences living among the Amish and their seemingly timeless world — a journey inspired by her fascination with Amish quilts. She lives in Berkeley, California, with her husband Richard, and is the mother of two grown sons.

YITZHAK BUXBAUM is a Jewish spiritual storyteller and teacher of Judaism. He is the author of five books. When a Jewish delegation visited India recently, a prominent rabbi gave Yitzhak's book about mysticism, *Jewish Spiritual Practices*, as a gift to the Dalai Lama. Yitzhak publishes the Jewish Spirit Booklet Series in which the first two volumes are *Real Davvening: Jewish Prayer as a Spiritual Practice and a Form of Meditation* and *An Open Heart: The Mystic Path of Loving People*. Yitzhak teaches at synagogues throughout the country and at The New School for Social Research in New York City.

JIMMY CARTER was the thirty-ninth president of the United States. He is the author of twelve books, including the national bestsellers *Always a Reckoning* and *Sources of Strength* and the acclaimed spiritual autobiography, *Living Faith*.

SHUMA CHAKRAVARTY is a global citizen who is a mystic, scholar, and minister. The main sources of inspiration in her life come from Vedanta philosophy of ancient India, mystical dimensions of world religions, and great literature. She worked for five years in the 1980s as a teaching assistant to Nobel laureate Elie Wiesel. Shuma was fortunate to have known Mother Teresa for many years and was blessed to have been greatly loved and inspired by her. Shuma is a minister of the First Parish Church in Dorchester, Massachusetts, a founding institution of Harvard University.

AVERY DULLES, S. J., is the Laurence J. McGinley Professor of Religion and Society at Fordham University and Professor Emeritus at the Catholic University of America. He is an internationally known theologian and lecturer, and the author of nineteen books and over six hundred articles on theological topics. Past president of both the Catholic Theological Society of America and the American Theological Society, Father Dulles has served on the International Theological Commission in Rome, Italy. He is a consultant to the Committee on Doctrine of the National Conference of Catholic Bishops and an associate fellow of the Woodstock Theological Center in Washington, D.C.

BROOKE MEDICINE EAGLE is a Native American earth wisdom teacher, singer, ceremonial leader, sacred ecologist, and author of *Buffalo Woman Comes Singing,* in which she explores Native American rituals like the medicine wheel. A Lakota raised on the Crow reservation in Montana, she is a licensed counselor, practitioner of Neuro-Linguistic Programming, and certified Feldenkrais practiner. She lives in the Flathead Valley of Montana, is the creator of Eagle Song, a series of spiritually oriented wilderness camps, and is the founder of the Flower Song Project, which promotes a sustainable, ecologically sound path upon Mother Earth for seven generations of children.

PAUL R. FLEISCHMAN, M.D., trained in psychiatry at Yale University, and is the author of *The Healing Spirit: Religious Issues in Psychotherapy* and *Spiritual Aspects of Psychiatric Practice.* He has been honored by the American Psychiatric Association for his contribution to the spiritual and humanistic side of psychiatry, and was the Williamson Lecturer in Religion and Medicine at the University of Kansas School of Medicine. He has given lectures and workshops at psychiatric and medical conferences and at colleges, churches, and interfaith societies. His love of poetic language led to the publication of his books *Cultivating Inner Peace* and *Kamma and Chaos: Collected and New Essays on Vipassana Meditation.* More information on Vipassana Meditation courses can be obtained at http://www.dhamma.org.

MAURICE FRIEDMAN is Professor Emeritus of Religious Studies, Philosophy, and Comparative Literature at San Diego State University; co-director of the Institute for Dialogical Psychotherapy; and on the faculty of the new non-denominational West Coast Jewish rabbinical seminary.

Among the more than twenty books that he has published are *The Worlds of Existentialism: A Critical Reader, Martin Buber's Life and Work* (3 vols.), *The Healing Dialogue in Psychotherapy, A Dialogue with Hasidic Tales: Hallowing the Everyday, Encounter on the Narrow Ridge: A Life of Martin Buber,* and *A Heart of Wisdom: Religion and Human Wholeness.*

BILLY GRAHAM has touched more lives with the good news of Christ than anyone in history. His famous crusades have taken him to every continent, and he has become a pastor and friend to heads of state throughout the world. Dr. Graham's best-selling books include *Approaching Hoofbeats, Angels, How to Be Born Again, Peace with God, The Holy Spirit, The Secret of Happiness,* and his autobiography, *Just as I Am.* He lives with his wife, Ruth Bell Graham, in the mountains of North Carolina.

DREW LEDER, M.D., PH.D., is an Associate Professor of Eastern and Western Philosophy at Loyola College in Baltimore. His recent book, *Games for the Soul,* teaches "the light-hearted path to enlightenment" — forty games for spiritual growth. His previous book, *Spiritual Passages,* explores the quest for wholeness in life's second half, using stories, teachings, and meditations from a variety of spiritual traditions.

ALBERT LOW has been practicing Zen since 1961. His first teacher was Yasutani Roshi, and he subsequently practiced with Philip Kapleau for twenty years, receiving transmission in 1986. In 1979 he was sent to Montreal where he has taught ever since. He is the author of eight books: *Zen and Creative Management, An Invitation to Practice Zen, The*

Iron Cow of Zen, The Butterfly's Dream, The World: A Gateway (commentaries on the Mumonkan), *To Know Yourself, Flowers of Air (Zen and the Sutras)*, and *Creating Consciousness*.

STELLA TERRILL MANN was member of the Unity School of Christianity and a widely published writer on the topic of Christian principles. Beginning in December 1943 and running for nine consecutive months, she published a series of articles in *Unity Monthly* magazine entitled, "How to Demonstrate," which refers to a metaphysical term meaning how to solve the problems of life by means of prayer. Later she revised and greatly enlarged the series and published it in her bestseller, *Change Your Life Through Prayer.*

ALAN C. MERMANN, M.D., M.Div., is a chaplain and clinical professor of pediatrics at Yale University School of Medicine. He received his medical degree from Johns Hopkins, and his Master of Divinity and Master of Sacred Theology from Yale University. He completed his residence training at New York Hospital and did his postdoctoral work in pediatric oncology at Sloane-Kettering Institute. He is an ordained minister and associate pastor of the Church of Christ Congregational, United Church of Christ in Norfolk, Connecticut. Dr. Mermann teaches a unique seminar on the experiences and needs of the seriously ill patient for first-year medical students in which each student is paired with a patient who serves as a teacher during the semester. In addition to counseling and teaching, he has written two books and forty-five articles and reviews for various journals.

SAMUEL H. MILLER (1900–1968) served as pastor of the Old Cambridge Baptist Church and as dean of the Harvard Divinity School. His many books include *The Life of the Soul, The Dilemma of Modern Belief, Man the Believer,* and *The Great Realities.*

LOU NORDSTROM is a Zen teacher (Sensei), receiving his Dharma Transmission from Bernie Glassman Roshi. He is the editor of *Namu Dai Bosa,* a collection of talks and memoirs by Nyogen Sanzaki, Soen Nakagawa Roshi, and Eido Shimano Roshi, and has just completed a collection of essays, *Opening the Throat,* which explores compassion and emotion in Zen.

HENRI J. M. NOUWEN (1932–1996) was born and educated in Holland, where he was ordained as a priest in 1957. He taught at the University of Notre Dame, Yale Divinity School, and several institutions in Latin America and Holland. He wrote several books including *Creative Ministry, The Wounded Healer, Aging,* and *Reaching Out.*

LEO J. O'DONOVAN was ordained as a priest in the Society of Jesus in 1966. He has edited five books, the most recent of which is entitled *Faithful Witness: Foundations of Theology for Today's Church.* He currently serves as a professor of theology and president of Georgetown University.

Since 1995 LLOYD JOHN OGILVIE has served as Chaplain of the United States Senate. Prior to that appointment he served as senior pastor of the historic First Presbyterian

Church of Hollywood in California, where his radio and television ministry, "Let God Love You," was broadcast throughout the nation. In 1988 he was named "Preacher of the Year" by the National Association of Religious Broadcasters. In February 1996, Dr. Ogilvie was recognized by Baylor University in a worldwide survey as one of the twelve most effective preachers in the English-speaking world. He is the author of more than forty books.

DALE EVANS ROGERS, actress, singer, speaker, and television and radio personality, has written several best-selling books, including *Angel Unaware*. She is the widow of popular cowboy star Roy Rogers. She lives in California.

JEFFREY BURTON RUSSELL began his exploration of prayer at an early age. He had been raised as an atheist, but at age ten he had an immediate and absolute experience of a Divine Presence. Later he became a religious scholar and published a number of books and articles on the history of theology, including five volumes on the history of the Devil and his latest book, *A History of Heaven: The Singing Silence*.

DALE SALWAK, a professor of English at Southern California's Citrus College, has taught courses and conducted seminars on biblical history and literature for over twenty-five years. He attended Purdue University (B.A., 1969), which awarded him its Distinguished Alumni Award in 1987; and the University of Southern California (M.A., 1970; Ph.D., 1974) under a National Defense

Education Act Fellowship. In 1985 he was awarded a National Endowment for the Humanities grant. Professor Salwak's works include eighteen books on various contemporary literary figures, as well as *The Wonders of Solitude, The Words of Christ,* and *The Wisdom of Judaism,* all published by New World Library.

CHARLES SPURGEON (1834–1892) became one of the greatest British preachers of all time. Coming from a flourishing country pastorate in 1854, he accepted a call to pastor the New Park Street Chapel in London, England. The chapel congregation soon outgrew its building and so, in 1859, work began on Spurgeon's Metropolitan Tabernacle, which eventually served a congregation of over 6,000. Spurgeon added well over 14,000 members to his congregation during his thirty-eight-year London ministry. His sixty-three volumes of sermons stand as the largest set of books written by a single author in the history of Christianity.

ANTHONY STERN, M.D., is the editor of *Everything Starts From Prayer: Mother Teresa's Meditations on Spiritual Life for People of All Faiths.* He has been a student of prayer for more than twenty-five years and has lectured on psychology and religion at the New York Open Center, the American Academy of Psychoanalysis, and many other settings. He works at Westchester Medical Center's Mobile Crisis Team as associate director and attending psychiatrist and serves as a consultant to Project Return's Starhill facility, an inpatient drug rehabilitation program in the Bronx.

MOTHER TERESA (1910–1997) became known around the world for her selfless work with the "poorest of the poor" in Calcutta, India. Born in Skopje, now the capital of Macedonia, Mother Teresa began her novitiate in India in 1928. Since its inception in 1950, her order, the Missionaries of Charity, has opened more than five hundred centers around the world to help the dying and destitute. Mother Teresa was the recipient of many of the world's most prestigious humanitarian awards, including the United States' Medal of Freedom, the United Nations' Albert Schweitzer Prize, and the Nobel Peace Prize.

NEALE DONALD WALSCH lives with his wife, Nancy, at Heart Light, a retreat site they have founded in the woodlands of southern Oregon. Together they have formed ReCreation, an organization whose goal is to give people back to themselves. Walsch is continually touring the country, answering requests for lectures, and hosting workshops to support and spread the messages contained in *Conversations with God*.

HAZEN G. WERNER is widely recognized as an authority in the field of pastoral counseling and as a leader in the Christian family life movement, which he has served in the roles of pastor, author, teacher. Since 1948, he has been a bishop of the Methodist Church. His publications include *Christian Family Living*, *Real Living Takes Time*, and *Your Family and God*.

DALLAS WILLARD is a professor at and former director of the School of Philosophy at the University of Southern California. He is an adjunct professor of spirituality at Fuller Theological Seminary and an ordained Southern Baptist minister.

MARIANNE WILLIAMSON is an internationally acclaimed author and lecturer in the fields of spirituality and new thought. She teaches the basic principles of *A Course in Miracles* and discusses their application to basic living. Her books *A Return to Love, A Woman's Worth,* and *Illuminata* have all been #1 *New York Times* bestsellers. Ms. Williamson is a native of Houston. She has been lecturing professionally on spirituality and metaphysics since 1983, both in the United States and abroad. She has done extensive charitable organizing throughout the country in service to people with life-challenging illnesses. Her latest book is *The Healing of America.*

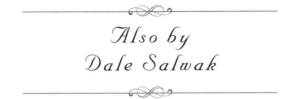

Also by
Dale Salwak

AVAILABLE FROM

NEW WORLD LIBRARY

The Wonders of Solitude. More than three hundred quotes that sparkle with meaning for the contemporary reader. A book everyone in our busy, noisy world can benefit from.

> "I highly recommend this book for those who want to live life to the fullest."
>
> — Lloyd John Ogilvie

> "Find a private, quiet place and indulge in this book."
>
> — NAPRA Review

The Words of Christ. This remarkable book distilled from the New Revised Standard Version contains the fundamental teachings of Christ arranged thematically to open up our understanding of familiar passages and to invite us to look more deeply within ourselves. A powerful reminder of where our traditions came from and of the great promises to us if we read and heed these words.

The Wisdom of Judaism. Dale Salwak plumbs the vast teachings of Judaism for its essence in this concise treasury of practical and inspiration Jewish insight. Includes an afterword of quotations from such modern Jewish thinkers as Albert Einstein, Golda Meir, and Margaret Fishback Powers along with an introduction by Rabbi Yechiel Eckstein.

Permissions

Grateful acknowledgement is made to the following for permission to reprint previously published materials:

Jimmy Carter and Times Books, a division of Random House, Inc., for "Pray Without Ceasing," excerpted from *Sources of Strength* (1997).

Paul R. Fleischman and Tarcher/Putnam for excepts from *Cultivating Inner Peace* (1997).

Billy Graham and Word, Inc., for "Effective Prayer," originally titled "The Power of Prayer," excerpted from *Hope for the Troubled Heart* (1991).

Stella Terrill Mann and Dodd, Mead & Company, Inc., Publishers, for "Praying for Power," excerpted from *Change Your Life Through Prayer* (1954).

Samuel H. Miller and Harper & Brothers Publishers, for "Prayer and Life," excerpted from *The Life of the Soul* (1951).

Henri J. M. Nouwen and Doubleday, a division of Bantam Doubleday Dell Publishing Group, Inc., for "The Paradox of Prayer," excerpted from *Reaching Out* (1975).

Lloyd John Ogilvie and Regal Books, for "Prayer Starts with God," excerpted from *You Can Pray with Power* (1988).

Dale Evans Rogers and Fleming H. Revell, a division of Baker Book House Company, for "Say Yes to God's Gift of Prayer," excerpted from *Say Yes to Tomorrow* (1996).

Charles Haddon Spurgeon and Whitaker House, for "Guaranteed to Succeed," excerpted from *The Power of Prayer* (1996).

Mother Teresa, for "On Prayer," excerpted from *No Greater Love* (1997).

Hazen G. Werner and Upper Room Books, for "The Family and Prayer," excerpted from *Your Family and God* (1962).

*I*f you enjoyed *The Power of Prayer*, we highly recommend these books from New World Library:

For the Love of God edited by Benjamin Shield, Ph.D., and Richard Carlson, Ph.D. In this wonderfully diverse collection of original writing, an extraordinary group of thinkers and teachers celebrate their personal experiences of the divine.

No Greater Love by Mother Teresa, with a foreword by Thomas Moore. This definitive volume features Mother Teresa on love, prayer, giving, service, poverty, forgiveness, Jesus, and more. The most accessible and inspirational collection of her writings ever published.

In the Heart of the World by Mother Teresa. A small book of Mother Teresa's inspiring words, divided into thoughts, stories, and prayers. Readers will learn Mother Teresa's philosophies, follow her as she works in the desperate corners of the world, and share her favorite prayers.

Small Graces by Kent Nerburn. Take a journey into the sacred moments that illuminate our everyday lives in twenty elegant pieces. Writer, sculptor, and theologian Kent Nerburn celebrates the daily rituals that reveal our deeper truths through the explanation of simple acts.

Simple Truths by Kent Nerburn. This profound book is deeply informed by the spiritual traditions of the West, the Far East, and the Native Americans with whom the author has worked. It is a small treasure of wisdom about life's deepest issues.

The Sacred Earth edited by Jason Gardner with a foreword by David Brower. Drawn from the great works of contemporary American nature writing, this profound and beautiful collection celebrates the earth and explores our spiritual relationship with nature.

New World Library
is dedicated to publishing books and tapes
that inspire and challenge us to improve the
quality of our lives and our world.

Our books and tapes are available
in bookstores everywhere.
For a catalog of our complete library
of fine books and cassettes contact:

New World Library
14 Pamaron Way
Novato, CA 94949
Tel: (415) 884-2100
Fax: (415) 884-2199
Or call toll-free: (800) 972-6657
Catalog requests: Ext. 50
Ordering: Ext. 52
E-mail: escort@nwlib.com
http://www.nwlib.com